CHAOS

TO PEACE

KATE CLARK

ISBN 978-1-64468-812-0 (Paperback)
ISBN 978-1-64468-813-7 (Digital)

Covenant Books, Inc.
11661 Hwy 707
Murrells Inlet, SC 29576
www.covenantbooks.com

To Jesus Christ, my Lord and Savior
To Chancy, the love of my life
To my posse

PROLOGUE

CHAOS /ˈkā-ˌäs/ NOUN, COMPLETE DISORDER and confusion; in physics, behavior so unpredictable as to appear random, owing to great sensitivity to small changes in conditions.

I was born into chaos, grew up to create my own chaos, and finally found peaceful chaos.

Would my life have been different had I known a personal relationship with Christ at an early age? Absolutely! But I wouldn't know that until years later. Throughout the following pages, you'll probably have mixed thoughts and feelings. Throughout these pages, lives a young woman with a joyful, innocent, curious, stubborn little girl inside. That little girl never left. She simply got lost in her desperate, although misguided, search for love. Pain led me down some interesting paths, ones I'd never have investigated had I known God at the time. In the end, I hope that's the message you come away with.

Over the years, many people have told me I should write a book. So now, at seventy-two years old, I sit in my recliner, recalling my life stories. Stories of emotional abuse, humor, adventures, stories of finding myself and finally finding happiness, stories that reflect my continual search for someone who could love me for the person I am, tales that show how far out of the norm I went in that search— all based on my perceived lack of love from my mother and to prove to my parents that I was the good person I knew I was.

As the character, Rabbi Eli from *Grey's Anatomy* once said, "Faith is not faith if you only believe when things are good." In the end, I find that to be true, but just how much do I endure in the process? This book will provide the answers.

CHAPTER 1

MY PARENTS, KATHERINE AND BEN, at age thirty-six and married for eight years, finally decided to have a child. My mother was very fearful that she wouldn't be a good mother—I think this must have been due to her own upbringing, although I can't be sure. Both of my parents were raised in matriarchal families, but my mother also had an extremely dysfunctional relationship with her sisters—Christina, nine months older, and Ruth, ten years younger. It was as though they were intertwined into one person forever more known as "the girls," thinking and acting alike in almost every situation. It felt to me and my cousins like being raised by three mothers. My dad was fun, easygoing, loving, and affectionate. Sadly, he was unable to stand up to my mother. In his relationship with my mother, he was passive. Because she had such a strong personality and a hair-trigger edge, overreacting at every turn, he stayed out of her way, letting her lead. He went quiet when Mom and I would argue. In one exception, he said to us when we were raving at each other, "Someday something will happen to one of you, and the other will feel very bad." He later told me he "didn't want to rock the boat" with her, so I was left to swim furiously alongside that boat. I often felt as though I were drowning, but somehow, I always kept my head above water.

Right away, I was a disappointment to my mother. Allergies to many formulas caused me as she remembered to "squeal like a little piggy and then throw up all over yourself." This, of course, was considered unacceptable because it didn't fit in with my mother's image of a perfect, beautiful child. It also caused me to be very cranky, and my mother took this as an indication that she was a poor mother—self-fulfilling prophecy. As I went through my childhood,

I was constantly told, not necessarily in explicit words, that I wasn't good enough. "You look nice, but…," "you did that, but…," always a "but" following any rare praise she would offer. When I fell off my bike at age five, I ended up with a huge scrape covering my right cheek. Instead of being worried about my physical well-being, she said, "What are we going to do? You're supposed to be a flower girl in just a week." Another memory I have is going with my mother to an open house at my kindergarten, and I overheard her telling my teacher while looking at my project, "Well, Kathy just isn't creative." That has stuck with me until this day. When my first-grade teacher told my parents that I responded well to praise, it was viewed as a weakness, and therefore, praise was withheld. Even my aunts told me, "Why do you need praise? We never did." I also got into trouble at age four because I went next door to my girlfriend's house. My mother was upset because then "the neighbors will know I'm still in bed." Always the one for outward appearances.

The character, Vivian, in the movie, *Pretty Woman*, tells her "John" Edward, "People put you down enough, you start to believe it."

"I think you are a very bright, very special woman," Edward tells her.

"The bad stuff is easier to believe. You ever notice that?" Vivian responds.

From my earliest memories, there were struggles with my mother. Her age at my birth was part of the problem, but the childhood she had created expectations for me. My mother wanted the perfect daughter. No daughter is perfect, of course. But it was as though she was saying, "look at what I've done," as she told others what I was doing. Sometimes I felt like an appendage. She was controlling of me and Dad, trying to form the family she may have dreamed of as a child. When we failed to meet those expectations, she could be vicious. She usually presented a very cold attitude that made affection from me difficult to give. I grew to understand that my mother had some serious psychological problems. But in those days, that subject was never discussed.

Katherine's priorities in the family were more about appearances to the outside world than the internal realities for Dad or me. My injuries, when they happened, were more of an issue about the neighbors and her friends. Her focus was misplaced. She was not concerned about how I was feeling, just how I would look to others. As I saw other parents in action or heard my friends describe their mothers' reactions to various things, I began to see how far from the norm my mother lived.

Strangely, my mother was interested in every detail of my life to the point of obsession. On the surface, one expects a mom with one child to dote. But Katherine's interest was more like espionage. What she found out about my school day or conversations with friends eventually worked against me. My mother wanted all the social details of my day and frequently told me that she was the only one to hold the role of "best friend."

My father, on the other hand, was sweet, caring, and kind. I have fond memories of him taking me to his office at Schlitz Brewing on Saturdays. I would sit at his secretary's desk, and he would give me something to type. Not having a clue of what I was doing, I would type away, giving him the unintelligible results. I still received his praise. He enjoyed showing me off to his coworkers. I cherished the moments there. Sadly, his one flaw was that he couldn't stand up to my mother for his own sake or mine. My mother would say, "My Willie can do anything," and she would frequently send him off to help her sisters with tasks. He went. She controlled him as tightly as she did me.

A very happy memory was learning to read with Grandma Larsen, Katherine's mother. While "the girls" experience with her might have been trying in their youth, I had a wonderful time as she coaxed me to read for myself. We'd sit on the settee, and she'd run her finger under the words as she read to me. She instilled in me a love of reading and a love of books. My dad's parents were never a priority, although they lived in the same city. This was due to Katherine's dislike for them, and her need to limit family to her own.

One day, when I was around four, my dad had chest pain while changing a tire and was rushed to the hospital with a potential heart attack. Thankfully, that wasn't the case, and I got to visit him in the hospital, even speaking to him over the intercom. I was totally fascinated with the care process, and I thought this was the best thing ever. That visit, combined with the fact that I enjoyed taking care of my grandmother when she lived with us, meant to my parents that I was destined to become a nurse. It never changed in their minds, and I just went along, believing this to be true. I was even given a nurse's uniform for Christmas and a doctor's outfit complete with medical bag for my birthday. My fate was sealed. At my mother's urging, I became founder and president of the Medettes in high school. It was a group of girls who had plans for a future in medicine, and we went to a variety of settings, even observing an embalming and an autopsy.

Katherine was an unstable swing of positives and negatives. You never knew what you were going to get. My mother was intelligent, frequently finding enjoyment in crossword puzzles and being interested in world events. In turn, she was self-conscious about having only an eighth-grade education. She had been fearful about becoming a mom but then attempted to control the natural chaos of family life with overreaching control. She never taught me to cook or clean, afraid that I would "make too much of a mess" or wouldn't do a thorough job.

Out from under the tough regime of my mother at home, my friends found me cute, talkative, fun, and smart. I had a circle of good friends—Patty, Barb, Cheryl, Janis, and Kathy. I enjoyed time with my cousins—Vaughn, who was eighteen months younger, and Stephen, who was six years younger. They lived with us for a year after their father battered my aunt, and a divorce followed. We would have fun putting on plays for the family and neighbors. Vaughn would become frustrated with me because I was bossy and wanted to rehearse when he'd rather play baseball. Vaughn would keep professional baseball scores on a blackboard, while Stephen and I made meals which consisted of leaves from our bushes. My impatient "mother" side sometimes showed up when I attempted to teach my much younger cousin, Stephen, to read. I remember being tough with him and yelling at him when he made mistakes. When I mentioned this to him when we were both much older, Stephen replied, "That was you who yelled? I thought it was Katherine." Stephen reported that he left the family because of my mother. At sixteen, he visited his dad in Miami where he had moved after the divorce. Stephen didn't want to go back to his mom and the sisters in Wisconsin. His dad tried to persuade him to return home, but he wouldn't go. He lived out his life in poor health and always believing he'd been a failure, dying while trying to prepare for Hurricane Harvey in 2017. His brother, Vaughn, ended his own life in 2016, outwardly successful but inwardly tortured. My dad, Stephen, and Vaughn were "the boys." Katherine and the aunts were "the girls," and that left me—where? I never felt like I belonged, and I was told that I frequently asked if I was adopted. Vaughn was the "golden boy." Stephen had been "brainwashed" by his father. My role, according to Vaughn, much later in our lives, was that of "scapegoat."

Several happy afternoons were spent at Milwaukee County Stadium, watching the Braves play baseball. Because of my dad's job, he'd frequently get free tickets, seating us directly behind home plate. No one wanted to sit next to Katherine because she'd grab the nearest knee, squeeze, and scream at her loudest, often for the other team. She was an embarrassment to all of us. At that time, the players' wives and children would sit in the section next to ours, and we were able to play with the likes of Billy Bruton's children, a famous Braves' pitcher.

We always went on an annual vacation with my dad driving and me navigating. We went all over the country, including Grand Canyon, Mount Rushmore, Washington, DC, and even lived in California for six months because of my dad's job. I attended first grade out there. Because Milwaukee schools were so far ahead of California ones and my reading was so good, I was left alone in the classroom to help my classmates with their words.

We all enjoyed the vacations, and my mom participated in everything. But there was one in Arizona when Katherine objected to a visit with Ben's sister. At sixty miles an hour, screaming loudly, she opened the back door with the supposed intent of jumping out. Dad reeled her back in, and then we went to visit his sister.

My grades were very good, and I even won a poetry contest. I remember being in Miss Burke's English class when President Kennedy was assassinated. That was a very surreal day for everyone. But in those days, I was only focused on surviving my own very difficult life. I didn't have the emotional energy to worry about or struggle with historical or world events.

I got my first period in history class when I was sixteen. I called my mother to tell her about this coming-of-age experience. It was an intimate story that I somehow thought might be a bonding moment with my mother as I took a uniquely feminine step toward adulthood. I thought it would be an experience with her that we would hold just between the two of us. She happened to be with her bridge club when I called her, and to my surprise and chagrin, she turned to her club while we were still on the phone and announced the arrival of my period to her friends with one of her isn't-that-cute little laughs. I felt very embarrassed, angry, and betrayed. On the other hand, I was strictly admonished not to tell anyone about the activity in our home. In retrospect, I believe that being chatty and sharing my ongoing story with my friends was the thing that saved my mental health. But time and again, I was chastised for revealing too much of the family's business. What happened at home was always to be kept secret unless Katherine decided it wasn't. She obviously believed that telling the other two-thirds of "the girls" was keeping a secret because they knew everything except her real part in the stories. Of course, they were accustomed to her control as well, but I'm not sure they ever understood the impact her behavior had on them or on me.

My dad was warm and loving, quick with the hug and kisses. Later in my adult life, he stopped over one day and said, "I just saw a bumper sticker that said, 'Have you hugged your kid today,' and I realized I hadn't hugged my kid in a while." Another warm and fuzzy moment with Dad. He had an open personality, genuinely interested in others not just in words but would go out of his way to help people. I remember his warm greetings to me. When I was little, I would see him come home from work and run down the driveway to him. He would pick me up and spin me around. It was a wonderful tradition while I was younger, and something I remember to this day. He was known as fair and honest at work. I've always tried to emulate these traits.

When he and I were interacting when my mom wasn't around, we always did well. He built me a foosball table from scratch. He enjoyed listening to me play the piano, even though I teased him that he always fell asleep. Dad had a great sense of humor that he exhibited when my mom was absent. He took walks with me, but they had to be short. When he returned from them, her active paranoia forced him to report everything in the conversation to my mother.

He was a kind man, always gentle and never swore. My father did spank me twice over the years. They were memorable occasions happening so infrequently since he was usually so laid back. Apparently, when I was eighteen months old, I enjoyed wandering through department stores. My parents would usually find me atop a jewelry case, responding to salespeople asking, "What does the lion say?" Finally, my dad told me that if I did it again, he would spank me. On the way home one afternoon, I kept asking, "Daddy, 'pank?" Daddy did. The other spanking is related further into the story. I was able to get out of the way of my mother's swinging attempts to hit me. She was awkward at it, and I became agile making a good defense by avoiding the smack. I never struck back, but embarrassingly, I must report that on one occasion, the screaming got so out of control on both sides that I suddenly realized I had my hands around her throat. I was horrified! Because she was older when my mother had me, I was too young to see the parent/child dynamics between her and her parents. I can only think that my grandparents were emotionally abusive toward my mother and her sisters in their youth. That may have caused them to believe the behavior to be the norm. "The girls" never spoke about their parents except to praise them to the point of making them saints in our eyes.

Education was important to my father. He'd left high school early but went back to graduate and continued his education as I was growing up. He was ever ready to help me with my homework, and one night, he stayed up all night to help me put together a project due the next day. He played games with me and taught me how to ride my bike. At State Fair, he would always ride the Wild Mouse roller coaster with me. He introduced to me the wonderful feelings of freedom even though they were brief. Ever after, as I tried para-sailing or any simple moment of freedom like wind blowing through my hair, I thought of him and his willingness to give me those little freeing moments in my youth. They were respites from my mother's hysterical, impulsive, and irregular parenting.

He praised me for my external good looks and the positive internal character traits he saw in me. This praise was so important to confirm the good and inspire me to continue to be a positive force in the world. But the fact that he was passive, where my mother was concerned, still led me to believe that she was right. It was clear that Dad was intelligent. He read a lot when he was around the house after work, and it was a terrific reinforcement of my growing love of reading when I was young. I watched him set up a budget, and he'd show me how it worked. Katherine couldn't or wouldn't understand the method and, therefore, took no interest. This was another bond my dad and I shared. I once had to teach her how to write a check.

He contributed to my finances being quite generous giving me cash when I was in dire straits. It was love that willed him to do it combined with my mother's nagging. He probably shouldn't have been so generous. It was too enabling, and it, therefore, took me until midlife to learn how to manage my own finances.

I loved school and loved any activity outside of the house. When I was with my friends, despite Katherine's instructions, I told them everything that went on at home with her. None of them could believe it was "that bad" until my friend, Kathleen, got caught in the middle of one of Mom's tirades. Kathleen never came back into our home again. She'd just pick me up outside in the car. My friends found me to be loyal, honest, loving, and a good listener. They also saw my sensitive, emotional side. I had a dog named Lady, a cocker spaniel that I adored. At about the same time, I wanted a bike of my own. My mom told me that if I wanted the bike, I had to give up my dog. This was "Katherine-logic." We found a farm where Lady could go and have a nice life. At the moment of giving her away, I was holding her and crying. I told my dog, "I love you so much," but again, I felt I had no choice. About two weeks after Lady was at the farm, she was hit by a car and killed.

I played piano for eight years, but when my teacher suggested I move my education to the Conservatory of Music in Milwaukee, I balked. I wanted to play show tunes, not classical music. I later regretted that decision. Although I've continued to have a piano in each of my homes, I've never played again because I'm too impatient (shades of Katherine) to practice.

"Traditions are stories families write together." I always wanted our family to have rituals and traditions. My friends had traditions like going to see the Nutcracker downtown at Christmas or to camp and family events every summer. Some had special times with their mothers baking cookies. My friends even played with their moms. I recall asking Katherine to play with me one day, but she had to "clean the house." I was crushed, and I didn't understand. Our house always looked like no one lived in it, so what was there to clean? My mother never let any traditions develop for some reason. At Christmas, I'd try every year to start some kind of tradition that related to the true meaning of the holiday. If it was allowed one year, it was stopped the next. If special moments happened, they happened chaotically and accidently, never recurring the same way again.

* * * * *

My mother and her two sisters, with whom she had a bond that probably had been forged in their own childhood were a force to be reckoned with for sure. The three siblings were inseparable and consistently shared the same opinions, especially where child-rearing was involved. However, perhaps due to being the only employed family member during the depression, Katherine was always looked up to as the leader. It was as if the three women had hard times in their youth and were in a survival pact emotionally, consciously or subconsciously, committed to backing each other up. The fact is that my mother and her sisters never shared any stories from their childhood, nor did they have pictures. I didn't find this odd at the time, but as an adult, I realized this too could show that there was something amiss during their childhood. They did talk a little bit about their early twenties, but that was all. Friends today find this hard to believe. The only story my dad shared was his *"job"* as a bootlegger, which is a strange occupation for someone like Ben. When my mother criticized me in front of Christina and Ruth, I could expect my aunts to side with and amplify my mother's rebuke. It was a devastating and relentless storm of women who frequently ganged up on me. I did, at one time, wish my dad had married Ruth, as I saw her as being more laid back. We'll find out if that was true further down the road. While the story of my mother's death is told later, the other two sisters died at ages eighty-nine and one hundred, two days apart, still mentally joined as if one.

My aunt, Christina, was the most unique one, a real character, compared to Katherine and Ruth. She was my grandmother's caretaker as Grandma aged. Christina remained single until she was fifty-two years old. She married a friend of the family, Al, who was a dignified, distinguished gentleman. In contrast, my aunt would run around in flannel pj's and a sweater with her stockings rolled down to her ankles. It was quite the sight.

Al was originally from England and was a widower. He and his deceased wife were both very social and elegant. I had no clue what he saw in my aunt, but he loved her until he died of emphysema three years later.

She would call me, quite disgusted, that two dogs who belonged to the policeman living behind her would copulate in her backyard. I could just imagine her moving from room to room to watch the dogs go at it and would complain later that it was just disgusting. My response was to 'just stop watching."

Christina would tell me some pretty strange stuff. She would advise me not to drink powdered dry milk because of all the rodent droppings in the mix. She had a very fertile imagination. She was very opinionated. Vaughn and I would bait her. We would bring up any issue from simple to complex, giving her a hypothetical situation and express an opinion. She would always take the opposite view. Then we'd switch our opinions, and she'd again argue the opposite side. We would disagree with her just to get her going. She also had a strict, rigid picture of whom we would marry—had to be Lutheran, white, and preferably Danish. Later in my life, when I was engaged to a Catholic man, she said she wouldn't come to the wedding.

On the flip side, since she lived in Racine, when I was eight or nine years old, I would take the train down to see her. She would make shrimp for me and let me stay up late watching movies with her. This was most enjoyable, making me feel particularly grown up.

After my first husband, Bob, died, she became less attacking and would invite me to a movie and worked to bring me back into the family after having married a Black man. Her kindness was clearly just a tactic to reclaim me, and it only lasted a little while.

During Mom and Dad's courtship years, my dad tutored Ruth in her high school subjects, and it's my opinion that she developed a crush on him.

Ruth married a very intelligent college professor. He moved with her to Madison, Wisconsin, to get her away from her family to ease the negative impact my grandmother, mother, and Aunt Christina would have on Ruth's personality. The professor tried to break the dysfunctional patterns he witnessed when they were all together. She continued to compare him to Ben.

On one occasion, my mother and grandmother went to Madison to visit Ruth and roasted her for the aesthetic choices she had made on some new furniture. Their criticism had such an impact on Ruth that she sent all the new furniture back to the store. The professor was not amused.

He subsequently took a teaching position in Florida where he could pursue his work as a marine biologist more ably and to put Ruth's family of origin even farther away. But Ruth's sisters had their emotional claws in her and the moves to Madison and to Miami had not ended the negative emotional ties. At one point, Ruth showed up on our doorstep, having been beaten by her husband. She arrived in the middle of a Halloween party I was having in the basement, so I had to send everyone home and tell them nothing. Of course, I told them everything.

My mom's comments to me about the professor colored my view of him, and I had lunch with him when I was on a college trip to DC, where he had taken a short-term government job. When I saw him, I ripped him "a new one" for beating my aunt. When I got home, my mom and my aunts were extremely angry with me, saying I shouldn't have confronted him but didn't explain why. Little did I know, I'd fallen into their dysfunctional pattern of thinking.

My parents supported Ruth when she came home to Wisconsin with her children and lived with us for a year. My mom and dad then bought them a house.

The strange dynamic between the three sisters was also in evidence when Christina went on the honeymoon with mom and dad. Ruth also went on the honeymoon with Christina and her husband. This honeymoon sharing wasn't the only strange behavior. The normal run of things for them was not to let one out of the sight of the other. As rigid and moralistic as they were, I'm sure nothing happened. They just shared the trips as we all did many times.

Another bizarre moment was when I was about ten, Ruth peeked through the bathroom door to watch me taking a bath and only using the bar of soap and my hands. She busted into the bathroom to finish the washing with a washcloth to do the job right. After that, there was no privacy for me. If I was on the toilet, my mother sat on the side of the tub. If I was in the tub, she sat on the toilet, chatting. When I was changing in my room, following a date, she followed. There was no getting away from her. Katherine told me that when "the girls" were young, they would always gather in the bathroom with their mother to discuss the details of their dates. I'm sure that's why my mom felt this was the normal thing to do.

A year and a half after my mother died, my dad married Ruth. At the time, it made sense to me, considering the family dynamics. For some reason, I still wasn't happy about it. Vaughn, on the other hand, moved out, telling me, "Finally, I don't have to take care of her anymore." I said to myself, "What was I thinking?" Even though I was out of the house, Ruth's behavior reminded me of mom. I would ask my dad if we could have lunch. We could meet just once a month, and that would be great. He would say, "I'll have to check." I would say, "If you don't do this for me, I'll know you don't love me." His decision to stay away was based on the thought that he had to live with Ruth. He didn't live with me. His compromise was that he would pop in for short visits. I was hurt and angry, having expected him to change, but also realizing he was unable to do so.

Eventually, Alzheimer's set in. When I asked him to fix something in my apartment, he cried. "All those years, I helped everyone else, and now I can't help my own daughter." It crushed him and broke my heart to see him like that. I'd visit him, and sometimes we'd have lucid conversations, sometimes not. One day, Ruth needed me because she wasn't feeling well. When I got there, Dad couldn't figure out how to let me in, but we finally found a way. She then decided to give me a key to the house in case something happened again. Several weeks later, she decided to take the key back. I was furious. For some reason, holding the key to someone's home meant trust to me, which then meant I was "back in the fold"), and she was now taking that away. It took me two weeks to get over any visit with my dad because she wouldn't let Dad and me visit alone at any time. That, and thinking he wouldn't know if I visited or not, I never went back.

Once I learned she'd placed him in a nursing home, I went to see him immediately. He recognized me, but he thought Vaughn, he, and I were going into the car repair business. I was supposed to put up billboards on the way home. I attempted to reorient him, and he pounded his fist on the table. "You never finish anything!" I assured him I'd put them up on the way home. There were only a couple more opportunities to visit him prior to his death, but I was pleased that Ruth did let me come to the hospital. I recall his beautiful blue eyes, his wavy white hair, and his sweet smile as we said we loved each other. He started to ask me a question, "Then why didn't you? Never mind." I now think he was going to ask why I'd never come to visit him, and it makes me sad, especially since I was too weak to handle Ruth and visit him, and she was too stubborn to call and tell me he was asking for me. Ruth stopped his life-maintaining medications, and every time I told him, "Jesus is waiting for you. We'll be okay," his blood pressure dropped, until after three times, he closed his eyes for the last time. It was very peaceful, just like he lived.

I'd always viewed Vaughn and I as remaining single, so I saw us being close and doing things together for the rest of our lives. When

I heard he was engaged, I was devastated, and instead of being happy, I selfishly sobbed before finally congratulating him. When Stephen got engaged, their dad told him, "You know you're marrying your mother." Stephen responded, "I know, but she's young, so maybe she'll change." Since his dad would be at the wedding, Ruth refused to attend. Sadly, the marriage ended in divorce after producing two boys of whom Stephen was very proud. Stephen had always wanted to be a veterinarian, but life put him on a different pathway. He was diagnosed with non-Hodgkin's lymphoma and had several complications from that but lived another twenty years.

Due to his extreme anxiety, he died of a heart attack while preparing to evacuate before Hurricane Harvey. My husband and I had visited him just four months earlier. Although we'd stayed in touch, we hadn't seen each other in twenty-five years, so that visit was especially important for me. Vaughn and Stephen's father, the professor, later married a professional woman and stayed in Florida until his death. He always viewed Ben as a hero for living with and tolerating "the girls" for all those years, and I'm sure he'd have chuckled at learning of Ben and Ruth's marriage. Vaughn died when he was sixty-six by his own hand. He was married with two children. He never told his wife about his past, and when Stephen asked to discuss something from their youth, his reply was, "That's in the past, we don't have to talk about it anymore." His wife is very nice and genuinely surprised when she hears of some of the details of our lives as children. However, she was always aware that Ruth's wishes were to be fulfilled. His kids are able and successful. Vaughn's career was in IT, and I was always very proud that he was my cousin and friend. It affected me deeply when he died.

When my mother attempted to show me love, it always came out in things bestowed not affection shared. After all, my mother and aunts couldn't wait to point to the things my mom and dad had given me when I'd question her love. They couldn't comprehend that I was bankrupt when it came to actual love. My emotional cup was empty while my mother was incapable of realizing that what I needed was her love. I needed pieces of her, not things. My behavior during my entire life was a cry for affection and help; for her, it was ammo.

One winter, I slipped on the ice a block away from home and broke my leg. I made the painful crawl up to an apartment house where a kind person allowed me to call home. After I told my mother what had happened, she said, "Can't you walk home? I have bridge club." I explained how incapacitated I was, and that there was no way I could get home under my own power. She still hesitated, expecting me to do whatever I could to prevent her bridge club event from being ruined. I tearfully let her know how badly I was hurt. Reluctantly and angrily, she eventually relented and came and got me. When she helped me into the house, her card group was more concerned about making me comfortable than she was.

In my adult years, I realized that many of my experiences in puberty were turbulent because they coincided with my mother's experiences with menopause. The convergence of these two life passages for us made the already difficult relationship between us even more combative. On the other hand, she would also give me dubious advice about boys, tossing her hair, and saying, "Just do this and that, just say this," to get a boyfriend. I never got the "respect yourself" conversation. Her advice was colored by her own success as a very popular young woman. She dated many popular young men, and she seemed to feel I was somehow defective when it didn't happen in my life. I always felt she thought I was not smart enough or good enough to get a boyfriend on my own.

In some ways, my teenage years were typical. There was excitement in attending basketball and football games that also gave the opportunity to check out the guys in my school. My dad taught me to drive. Driving, biking, skating, the wind blowing through my hair, convertible rides with friends past boys' houses, hoping for a glimpse of them, all made me feel free for a little while, still caught in the prison of my family experience.

In mixed company, my usual openness reverted to a shy affect. I never felt like I was dressed right, and Mom's negative voice was always in the back of my head, squashing any positive thoughts about what I might do. She discouraged me from joining clubs where, in relaxed settings, boys and girls could get used to being around each other, and friendships could develop naturally. My friends had great experiences, finding lifelong friends among the opposite sex, even if they didn't find a romantic relationship, and they had fun.

Although claiming to be a Christian, even going to church was oddly corrupted by my mother. During worship, Katherine would scan the group, looking for potential boyfriends in the congregation for suitability. She critiqued what the other girls were wearing. Seeing something she liked on another girl, she would say, "See, now that's what you should be wearing." This hurt frustrated me too since my mother controlled clothing purchases, but I got the blame without having any power to improve my look. Besides, I always thought I looked pretty good until she shared her opinion. Nonetheless, I did have friends in the church, participated in the youth group, and I played the piano for the Sunday school, as well as teaching Sunday and summer Bible school. I was baptized as an infant and later went through confirmation classes but went through them numb—something one did when one was thirteen years old. Baptism and confirmation were important parts in starting my faith journey, but it wasn't fulfilled until a much later time.

My high school boyfriend's name was Bill. He was tall, lanky, and white. My friend, Eileen, and I bowled together. She was dating Bill at the time. When the Turnabout Dance came up in the school year, I was looking for a date. Turnabout was when the girls asked the boys to a dance. Eileen happened to be grounded by her parents. She suggested I take Bill to the dance. When he later asked me out, I went, and after that, we were inseparable. I stole him from Eileen. At the time, I didn't see it that way, but that's what it was, and Mom, of course, thought it was wonderful that I was "good enough" to take him away from her. Eileen never really recovered from my theft of Bill from her at the time. But years later at our forty-fifth high school reunion, she said, "Well, I guess we might as well get it out, what's between us, Bill." I couldn't believe she'd held a grudge for all those years, and I just walked away.

The summer between freshman and sophomore year of college, Bill and his family invited me to go with them on a camping trip to Yellowstone National Park. Our parents got together to talk about the trip to make sure I would never be in a compromised position. Satisfied, my parents let me go.

We were gone ten days pulling a camper as our housing for the trip. Bill, myself, his younger sister, brother, and his parents made up the traveling party. The trailer camper folded out and had sleeping areas for all of us. I had never been camping before, but it turned out to be a fun week. We did touristy things on the way like stopping at Wall Drug and the Corn Palace and the like. Seeing Yellowstone was great. Bill fed all of the bears he could find, although it was dangerous. His sister was extremely jealous of me. She wasn't used to sharing her big brother with another girl. She wasn't friendly to me at all. One morning, in frustration, she dumped a glass of milk over my head. I ran after her to get even, but she was bigger than me. Her parents ended up handling it. Bill and I got along great, feeling free to hold hands and share hugs. Other than his sister, the memory of the trip was a general happy glow.

He was my first kiss and my first love. My mom would annoy me by flirting with him. Even her sisters agreed that she "made a fool of herself." She also made it a habit to drive by his house whenever she and I were out together. She just wanted to see if he was home or if he was possibly cheating—how she expected to know that was never clear to me. I made sure I liked whatever he did. During my freshman year in college, he, his mom, and Katherine drove up to St. Olaf. Bill and I went to the big formal dance, and they spent the weekend. It was a memorable time. One day, during sophomore year, I decided to pull off a surprise visit at Whitewater where he was in college. But I got the surprise learning that he had another girlfriend. Her roommate was ecstatic that I'd come and said that Sue would be so disappointed to have missed me. Bill and I wrote a few letters after that, and I just couldn't adjust to the fact that he'd cheated on me.

When I got back to Milwaukee, I contacted him. We drove to Hansen's Golf where we had our first kiss, and I sobbed and begged him not to break up with me. He was somewhat compassionate but ended up informing me that he and Sue were getting engaged in two weeks. Exactly two weeks later, we had one final contact when he came to my house the day after he got engaged. When I met him at my door, we talked, and then I heard his fiancée coming up the driveway. He admitted she was still curious to see what I looked like. How tacky! I just slammed the door in his face. They eventually did marry.

CHAPTER 2

WHEN I WENT AWAY TO college, the weight of my difficult childhood compromised the advantages of being away, making new friends, and discovering myself as most students do. Most of the four years were a blur. Due to what I now recognize as depression, I slept through school much of the time. My grades even got so low that I was placed on probation. It would've been fine with me if I were to have been expelled, but unfortunately for me, I was only suspended. So I stereotypically pulled myself up by the bootstraps and got myself back on track. Although I had friends, my low self-esteem was also a problem. I was only accepted to a new sorority, the one for losers, while Amanda, my roommate and best friend, was accepted in the popular one. I was happy for her, but I couldn't figure out why I hadn't been chosen when we were so much alike. We did everything together like meals, chapel, social activities, and many lengthy conversations about life in general. We were like sisters. Where you saw Amanda, you saw Kathy. Actually, we did everything together—meals, chapel, social activities. We were like the sisters; both of us had always wanted. We spent breaks and weekends at each other's homes.

During our freshman year of college, my roommate, Amanda, came home with me one holiday. The airlines were giving away sample packs of cigarettes. We went to the park and stand in the cold, blustery weather so that my mom wouldn't smell the smoke in the car. Amanda didn't like smoking, but unfortunately, I did, and that began for me a long period of heavy smoking. I saw that her family was similar to mine, but more peaceful. We thought alike, laughed at the same things, and enjoyed the same activities. But going places alone, such as the library, was out of the question, at least for me.

One time, I had a paper due the next day, and I refused to go to the library if Amanda didn't accompany me. She finally did after much cajoling on my part. In looking back, the only thing we didn't really discuss was God, even though we went to daily chapel and Sunday church. Going to a Lutheran college, I just assumed we both believed the same things about him. I didn't learn until many years later that she already had a personal relationship with Christ.

I had several crushes during my years at St. Olaf College, but none of them came to fruition. While my roommates dated, I sat in the dorm and wrote letters to my friends. One nursing semester was spent off campus in the Twin Cities of Minneapolis/St. Paul at the VA hospital. Psychology was very interesting to me and followed me into my professional life, sometimes to my detriment. When my parents took me back to school prior to my junior year, I recall sitting in the park on a sunny, blue-skied fall day. And there I was, sobbing, begging not to return, but they were adamant that I continue, and of course, I had no choice. I'd had a great job in human resources at Continental Can Company during the summer, and they'd offered me a full-time position which I desperately wanted to take. Again, not an option. I had a wonderful nursing roommate, Karen, who made things better, and we stayed good friends until her death from breast cancer in the eighties. Over one Easter break, I went with her to visit her parents in Washington, DC. I was amazed, as we sat at the dinner table, that her parents discussed things with her as if she were a real person with real adult opinions. When I glowingly reported on my visit, my mother became very jealous and threw it in my face many times.

Finally, in my junior year, my mother's dream of me getting my "MRS degree" seemingly came true, and I met Jeff. We met on the bus returning from an away football game. He was a jokester, and we flirted while my roommate and I sat in front of him. He later asked me out, and we dated for about three months. I learned from a class-mate that we'd broken up. It hurt to learn that way. A man named Tom called to ask me out. I knew who he was, as prior to graduation, he'd been a big man on campus, captain of the football team and president of his fraternity. Besides that, he was tall, handsome, blue-eyed, and blond. Needless to say, I was thrilled. I was told that a guy in my class had suggested he call me. In reality, Jeff had told him about me. When I learned what had really happened, it made me furious that he would think he had to find me a boyfriend. I finally told him why I was so upset. We talked and became friends again. One night, he called, drunk, to see if I wanted to go to a concert with him. I did, and because we'd no longer been a couple for a while and I was now dating Tom, we sensed the crowd grow quiet as we walked to our seats down front. We found that curiously funny.

I dated Tom over the year that followed. My female friends at St. Olaf were excited because of who he was. He had already graduated and would come to St. Olaf to see me from the Twin Cities. We did a lot of things. He called every night, and one time, he took me to the Playboy Club.

Interesting experience. My mom adored him. One time, he stayed over at our house in Milwaukee when I wasn't there, and my aunts were horrified that he visited overnight because my dad was away on a business trip at the time.

He was a skier and took me skiing. In an attempt to please and catch him for me, Katherine bought me the ski clothes I needed, skis with bindings, and boots. He was annoyed when I was slow to learn, so he took off to another more challenging hill. In my learning process, I accidentally left the ski trail and went off a cliff. I flew through the air like a pro, and I actually landed on my feet. Unfortunately, he wasn't around to see that experience, but I was really proud of myself; plus, I once again enjoyed the feeling of freedom as I flew through the air.

On the evening before I graduated from college, we went on a "blanket party," and he told me that "God would want us to make love." I shoved him off and refused, responding, "God definitely doesn't want us to make love." On a couple of occasions, he gave me roses, and I met his parents, very kind and pleasant, welcoming me into their home. His father was a doctor, and that impressed Katherine to no end. During the time I knew him, I lived in Eau Claire, working in a pediatrics unit for a year. Tom would come in from Green Bay to see me, and one time, I called in sick to see him and got caught. Tom eventually took a job in Cincinnati and invited me to visit for a weekend. The morning after I arrived, he brought me flowers from his garden and made me breakfast in bed. Before he left for work, in the extreme romance of the moment, I lost my virginity with him. Katherine was okay with me going and not surprisingly with what eventually happened. It was almost as though she'd expected it, thinking, of course, it would lead to marriage. What a catch! A week later, he called to tell me he wouldn't be seeing me anymore. I was devastated.

I called my good friend, Jeff, who had introduced us, and he came to Eau Claire from St. Olaf. He listened to me cry and talk, and he spent the night on the floor next to my bed, holding my hand. The support and compassion he showed me continues to hold a special place in my heart.

As with the previous three years, my senior year was filled with daily letters from my mother. One in particular has stayed with me because it represented our relationship so well. It contained only questions, and they were actually numbered. One of them was, "Did you wear a slip under your yellow dress?" Pretty much says it all.

Several of my summers during my college years included very special experiences.

Between sophomore and junior college years, I worked at Continental Can, a large factory, as a human resources assistant. It was a very positive experience for me. My boss and many others thought I looked like Doris Day, an actress at the time, and he often called me by that name. At the age of nineteen, I found that very flattering.

One day, a man came to the counter in the department, and I asked if I could help him.

"Yes, would you like to go see the movie, *Sand Pebbles*, with me?"

I was stunned to say the least as his request had come out of the blue. Up until that time, my type was tall, well-built, handsome, intelligent, and white. A couple were thinner or heavier, but in general, they were the little white girls' dream in those years. Art was gorgeous, tall, well-built, intelligent, and black!

His father was a doctor. Other than that, I knew nothing about him.

"I'll have to think about it," I told him. The civil rights riots were going on at that time in Milwaukee, and my parents made it very clear that they viewed blacks as being equal to whites. Nonetheless, for some reason, I felt I needed to pass this by them. I went home and discussed his invitation with my mom. Surprising to me, in this particular case, she thought the date might not be a good idea. He came back into the office the next day, and I told him my parents didn't think we should go out. I never saw him again. Regret number one.

Surprisingly focused when motivated, Katherine somehow managed to have several adult friends. I was stunned to be told by many neighbors at one block party when I'd moved back to the neighborhood, how "wonderful" my mother was. She was kindhearted to everyone outside the family, but I was rarely the recipient of such kindness.

CHAPTER 3

IN THE FALL OF MY junior year in college, my roommate, Amanda, and I applied and were accepted to the International Summer School Program in Oslo, Norway. When Amanda transferred to another college for a semester, she was unable to make the trip. Being the person I was, seemingly unable to do things alone, I decided I wouldn't go either. However, my parents and friends convinced me that I'd miss out on a great opportunity, so I went. College, grad students, and other young adults from all over the world participated. My parents drove me to Washington, DC, where the plane was to depart. We thoroughly enjoyed the time, seeing all the sights. On the plane, I sat next to a girl with the same last name. We talked and laughed and decided to room together at the university. There was a lot of alcohol and food on the flight, so we all had a good time. The university itself was modern and colorful. All the buildings were bright colors and elevated on pillars to protect it from floods. There were several buildings separated by an open brick square with benches. We had classes in the morning in Norwegian literature, Norwegian language, and Norwegian history. I don't have a lot of memories about the academics. The social life was everything. There was no houseparent in our dorm, and each quad consisted of two very small rooms with a double bathroom in between. It was drab, but we made the best of it. Our quad mates were from Texas and North Dakota.

While there, I dated a man from America named Al who planned to live in Norway after graduation with a major in architecture. He also intended to give up his United States citizenship. We were inseparable for three weeks. We took long walks in Frogner Park with its many beautiful stone statues depicting all the phases of love.

It was impressive. I saw *Planet of the Apes* with him. Interesting to watch a movie in Norwegian with English subtitles. We walked along a beach and around the city for three hours on a sunny summer day. Suddenly he realized he was in love with me, asked me to marry him, realized we'd only been dating for three weeks, and never talked to me again, despite my attempts to contact him.

I also dated a man from Iran named Jim, third in line to the Shah. He'd decide he needed more clothes, would call home, and the next day, six silk suits would arrive. I was in awe. He was a very intelligent man, having been educated at the University of North Carolina in the United States. He was also very funny, kind, and handsome. We had wonderful times together. My dad must have heard me talk about him enough that he wrote a very succinct letter telling me, "Don't overdo." Jim wrote back, saying that I was an adult and could overdo but that I hadn't.

My dad was not amused. The long arm of my mother also reached Oslo in daily letters, asking every question imaginable. If I missed a few days of writing, she called to find out how things were going. Much later in my life, Jim came to the US to visit the chancellor of the university he'd attended. He called to invite me to visit. I already had a week's vacation planned at that time to go to St. Paul, so I told him no. He pleaded with me to change my plans, saying he'd pay for everything, and that I'd be staying at the chancellor's home. Regret number two. I think I said no because I might fail to take my dad's advice and overdo, plus I learned from letters from him that he was married and had a baby. I continued to refuse, and I never heard from him again. I wonder to this day what would have happened, even though I know it was the right decision. When the Shah was deposed by the revolutionary guard in Iran, my friend was probably caught up in the change. But having severed ties with him, I'll never know how his life turned out.

I celebrated my twenty-first birthday in Oslo, and Sethi, an Iraqi friend, took me to the Grand Hotel for a sumptuous dinner. The hotel was filled with gold, including gold-rimmed plates and silverware. I tasted champagne for the first time. It was a glorious way to spend such a major birthday. My roommate and I, with all our friends, spent a lot of time in the beer gardens. There were colorful umbrellas over the tables. It was airy and fun, and we'd discuss all sorts of topics from politics to gossips. The weather was perfect for it. Another memory is that of a little girl walking with her parents, totally naked except for a pair of red patent leather shoes. Adorable! We found a Coca-Cola machine at the bottom of the hill by the university, and for some reason, we found this ironic, a bit of home. There was a little train that led to the center of Oslo so that was always a fun ride, especially running to catch the last train at the end of the day. At this time, my roommate and I met black Norwegian twins while walking down the street. They wanted to take us out, so we set up a day and a time. For some odd reason, we got scared and didn't show up. They kept calling us and trying to reschedule and to find out why we didn't show. There was some unspecified fear, but we had no identifiable reason. We just never replied.

My roommate and I decided to hitchhike our way to Sweden without considering the distance or the potential dangers. We saw small, intricately designed churches. The sun shone through the windows throwing color everywhere, and the effect was just gorgeous. The hills, fjords, and general scenery were magnificent. We found a cute little blue and white motel and spent the night there. The room had twin beds and no indoor plumbing, but it worked for us in the moment. We continued our journey in the morning, meeting nice people along the way. As we hitchhiked on our way, we ran into a man who offered us a ride in his car. We got in the back seat, despite it being littered with empty beer bottles. He kept saying something in Norwegian that sounded like "my place," and Linda and I held hands and talked through gritted teeth, so he couldn't see us in his convex rearview mirror. We finally escaped at a red light in the center of town. Having escaped, we went to a restaurant with a black slate menu that said, "fish supper." We thought that sounded good, but it turned out to be cold fish soup that was pretty nasty. At dusk, we were hitchhiking again when two guys came up to us with ponytails, backpacks, and skulls hanging from them. They just asked us for cigarettes, but when we had none, they walked away. It was at that point that we decided to hitchhike back to Oslo.

When the international school ended, the city threw a party for us. There were many enormous tables of sweets, bread, meat, and amazing desserts to sample and fill your plate for the meal. There were champagne fountains. It was unbelievably extravagant.

I left Oslo on the train, in my own single compartment, for Bottrop, Germany, to visit my college roommate's AFS sister, Marianne, who took me, with several of her friends on the town, partying. Her parents didn't speak much English, but they welcomed me nonetheless, and Marianne and her little brother translated. They had the most wonderful down mattress, duvet, and pillows on my bed. I felt like a princess!

Once again, I took the train alone from Germany. I recall Koln as we passed through, looking out the window to see rain, clouds, and black church spires coming through them. In Copenhagen, I met up with Jim, the man from Iran and many of our other friends. We saw Tivoli gardens. It was lovely at night with tiny lights in all the many trees, but it was smaller than I'd expected. I also saw the statue of the Little Mermaid. I was underwhelmed by the experience as I had to stand at the top of a small knoll and look down at it. She looked very tiny. We walked along the boardwalk and saw the red-light district. While at a castle, I attempted to get the attention of one of the stern-faced guards to no avail. I waved my hand in his face, made weird faces, jumped up and down, etc. Oh well, let's just take a picture of me with him. As the picture was being taken, he suddenly jutted his hip out to bump me, winked, and resumed his rigid pose. I laughed.

All my ancestors are from Denmark, so it was good to visit there. Unfortunately, I couldn't locate any of my relatives.

My dad, Ben, knew the vice president at the brewery in Copenhagen. His secretary called to see if I'd like to spend the day with a Danish family, and I supposed it was her family. So I was more than a little surprised when a limo pulled up to my hotel. I thought, *Wow, if my friends could see me now!* The driver took me to a beautiful home, where I learned it belonged to the vice president himself. His daughter took me to see the countryside and several castles. It was all a little intimidating but nice. I had dinner at their home and met the brewery's vice president. I felt self-conscious because I knew I was representing my family and the US. He and his family were very gracious and put me at ease. Fortunately, my dad wrote a note of thanks for their generosity, which I regretfully, did not.

The trip gave me insights into people. I could put faces to those from other countries and realize they were just like me. Stereotypes didn't work with the people I met. I kept in touch for a long time with people from France, Norway, Iran, Iraq, plus my American friends. Being the kind of person who wouldn't do anything alone, I wonder how I could have been brave enough to do all the things I experienced. But it made for some self-confidence and a little pride in myself, and it sure was fun. My aunts later blamed the trip for my "negative behavior."

CHAPTER 4

IN MY EARLY TWENTIES, I did have the help of a psychiatrist. Even in this experience, my mother revealed her struggles while reluctantly attending one of my sessions. I remember the doctor asking my mother in a joint session, "Is Kathy always wrong?" My mother believed in her own brokenness as if he had said, "You are never right." She refused to return, despite the explanations and corrections Ben and I gave. My doctor understood what I was dealing with.

In my mid-twenties, I moved home after the death of my first husband, whose story will be told later. On my twenty-fifth birthday, Jeff had sent me a card referring to me becoming a quarter of a century. For some reason, that hit me hard, and on the way home from work, I started crying.

As I walked in the house with a tear-stained face, my mother's immediate response was, "Did you kill someone?" On one occasion, my father, Ben, had taken a day off from work to help his mother with something she needed. My mother was jealous, saying, "You never take a day off to do something with me." Things escalated quickly on her side, and she slapped my dad across the face, breaking his glasses and cutting his nose. He spent his only night away from home at the YMCA. I wondered if he'd return.

I remember one night, we were all tucked in beds when out of nowhere, my mother yelled out to me, "Do you realize your dad hasn't touched me in two years?"

"Who can blame him? You treat him like a damned dog," I replied.

In the next moment, she was diving at me with her hands around my throat, choking me. Dad pulled her off.

On another occasion during a time when my mom had been talking about suicide, Dad was at work, and I was sunning myself in the backyard. It was not uncommon as she came out the back door to scream at me and to go back in, slamming the door. She had screamed at me for something I had supposedly done. She then screamed she was going to kill herself, slamming the door shut again. For one brief second, I thought about staying where I was, but then I got up to go in after her, and the house was locked. I ran next door to the neighbor's house, and she remembered a key we had in the garage, and she got into the house and found Katherine in the basement standing on a chair with a rope around her neck as I was calling my dad at work. By the time I got back into the house, the neighbor had calmed her down and put her to bed. Mom's first comment to me was, "Why did you have to get the neighbor involved?" I was livid.

Dad came home in a company car, so I had to drive him back to get the car back to work. But we were worried to leave her alone.

"It's okay. I'll be all right. I'll make supper," she said sweetly like nothing had happened.

I was furious that she could put me through that and then turn on the charm as if all was normal.

When she was sixty-four, my mother had a fatal cerebral aneurysm. It was Easter, and I'd decided not to join the family for dinner as we always did, and that upset Katherine. For that reason, my aunts, until the day they died, blamed me for her death. That night, I was at home, exhausted from a long day. When the phone rang for the third time in a row, I decided I'd better answer it. My dad was calling to tell me they were taking Katherine to the hospital via ambulance. I could hear her in the background screaming from the severity of the headache. He also reported she'd been vomiting, and I thought this was all due to a massive migraine. I left the house immediately, heading for the hospital. I beat the ambulance, and when I saw her wheeled in, I knew this was no ordinary migraine. She coded in the emergency room, and they were able to stabilize her and get her to ICU. My dad and I were talking to her at the bedside. She'd always told me I'd probably "dump her in a nursing home." So I told her I loved her, and that I'd take care of her when she was better, knowing that her condition was grave. She said, "Oh, Kathy," which to me meant, "Oh, Kathy, why were you such a disappointment." Then she suddenly turned her head to the side, began labored breathing, and coded. We were escorted out immediately. Eventually, the doctor came out to tell us that she had no brain function, even though her heart was still beating. My dad looked at me and said, "You know what I want, I just can't say it." So at twenty-eight years old, I had to tell the doctor to let my mother go peacefully. The aunts were present, but not within hearing distance, and my dad and I agreed to keep this between the two of us. He eventually told Ruth, and I again felt betrayed. As we left the hospital, my aunts and dad walked together with me ahead and alone. Not unlike life, he with the aunts and me on my own. From 10:30 p.m. to 2:30 a.m., that's all it took for the family to be irreversibly altered. The next day, I called a friend whose mother had died of cancer exactly the year before. He said he just couldn't handle coming to the funeral home, and I understood.

At the visitation, the night prior to the funeral, I assumed people who knew my parents would come to offer sympathy. The first person to arrive was one of my coworkers. Someone who had come just to see me. I was amazed and overcome. Other friends and colleagues arrived, and some of us went downstairs to be together and to have a cigarette. I was chastised by my aunts for not being upstairs with the family. We had arranged it to be a closed casket service at her request. Vaughn sobbed as the family saw her for the last time. I believe he was mourning the loss of the reality he'd wished for. It was a simple service, and I cried, but I think I was more worried about my dad and how he was doing. Following the service, I turned around, and there was my friend, who—despite his own grief—had come to be there for me. A true friend. I immediately went to him, and when I turned back, the casket had been taken out of the funeral home. I let out a wail because I had wanted to say one final goodbye before they took her from the building. My dad and "the boys" had to help me in my distress.

The months that followed my mother's death were difficult for me. I stayed away from the family as much as possible because the remaining girls blamed me for Katherine's death. Because I hadn't gone to Easter brunch, they felt that her extreme disappointment caused the aneurysm. No amount of medical explanations would change their opinion. When I told my doctor, he said, "Consider the source." At that point, I only had my history with Katherine and her very loud voice in my head. There was a sense of betrayal. There was no way to improve or work on our relationship. There was no way I could finally win. The finality of our brokenness was a heavy burden.

Beyond these incredibly crucial realities, I happened to be in a relationship with a man who was mentally and emotionally abusive to me, despite my efforts to make something of this relationship. He was leaving to go out of town, and that felt like betrayal at the time too. I begged him to stay, but he refused. You'll learn a great deal more about him further in the book.

That afternoon, I wrote a note to my dad, my boyfriend, Tyrone, and my best friend, Jean, and left them on the table. I took an overdose of pills washed down with a lot of Jim Beam. When I didn't die fast enough, I decided I should call my friend, Grace, in Illinois to say goodbye. Grace and I had been friends since we were fourteen and met at church camp in Wisconsin. We'd stayed in touch over the years, becoming closer during critical times in our lives. I don't know what I thought she was going to do, but fortunately, she had Jean's phone number. She came to my apartment and called the paramedics.

When I was going down the hallway to the ambulance with the friend who saved my life, I screamed at her, "Jean, why are you doing this to me?" She said later that she almost told the ambulance attendants to take me back to my apartment.

I was in a coma for two days with the doctors concerned that I might have damaged my brain. My suicide attempt seemed to me to be the perfect response to the life my mother had given me. Mel B, in her autobiography, *Brutally Honest*, says "If you feel emotionally abused—whether it's a partner, a boss, even a parent—you can't see any scars, but they go way deeper, right down to your very sense of self. I felt empty, worthless." That is a perfect description of how I felt.

When Tyrone returned home from his weekend trip to find out I'd attempted suicide, none of my friends would tell him where I was or how I was doing. He mustered up the courage to call my dad and learned that I'd be okay. My dad, as always, was very gracious and told him where I was, so Tyrone called me. He told me I didn't need a psychiatrist for this, and I agreed, hung up the phone, and made the appointment with a psychiatrist.

At the time, I had no way to see the resilient core of the personality that I had created. My friends were true ones and knew the good and the bad of my life and still wanted me in their lives. While I was in the hospital, I had an LPN who took care of me when I was not yet quite conscious, yet she had experience with abusive partners. She put a note in my robe with her phone number inviting me to call and to talk. It was good to know someone cared about me. Dad and "the girls" came to visit me, and Dad took me home from the hospital. After that, I didn't hear a word from them, not even to check up on me. They'd gone to see my psychiatrist to see what they could do for me and he told them, "Nothing anymore." They understood that to mean they should just stay out of my life, and they did.

At some point after my mom died, I decided to have a family Thanksgiving at my place, and I decided to make everything myself even though I wasn't a cook. I had ham, turkey, all the sides, and several different desserts. I was so proud of myself. I had everything set up in the living room, and I was excited. It was my dad, his mother, Ruth and Christina, and Vaughn. I ended up being sorry. The very first thing Christina said when she walked through the door was, "Do you realize your sheer curtain is hanging backward?" She then walked over to the piano. "Oh, Ben, there's a candle on the piano. Shouldn't there be a coaster under it?" Vaughn and my dad were the only ones who were complimentary about the meal. The rest made pleasant little comments. As we were cleaning up afterward, Ruth and Christina went through my cupboards and expressed their opinion that I had entirely too many glasses. I almost told them what I thought but managed to keep my cool until they left.

One of the men in my life was Les. When I was four, I remember jumping on the bed with him, playing tag and doing things that four-year-olds do. He was nine months older than me. I always wanted an older brother. Our mothers thought it was great that we would be friends too, making it a three-generation history of friendship between the two families. Our grandparents were friends, as were our parents and the aunts. I had had a crush on him from the time I was four years old until I was twenty-one. However, I have no memories of interactions with Les during middle and high school. He hardly spoke to me then. I looked forward to every hello I got. My feelings for him were very unrequited.

When my friends and I went to YMCA dances, I could see him across the room. His girlfriend, Jeannie, would be sitting on his lap. Somehow, I convinced myself that he would be better off with me. My best friend got tired of hearing me talk about him. She saw things as they really were.

One day, when we were teenagers, Les was at our house. He was playing his trombone. We were laughing and having fun. Les accidently bumped a floor lamp with the slide of his trombone. Nothing was broken, and no one got hurt. My dad heard the noise of the collision, misread the situation, came into the room, and summarily sent Les home. Before Les was even halfway home, my dad took down my pants and spanked me for a perceived transgression.

"Wait, wait, wait," I said.

Dad stopped.

"What?" he said.

"Nothing happened."

He rejected my explanation and continued the spanking.

When I was a junior in college, I came home to surprise my mom for her birthday. I couldn't reach my parents, so I called Les, who happened to be home on leave from the navy, to pick me up at the airport. After that, we corresponded for a while, and he asked me out the next time I came home. I was thrilled and ran screaming up and down the halls of my dorm, but it was probably the worst date either of us ever had.

He backed his car out of his driveway across the street. He never opened the door to the car. I just walked out the door of my house and got in the car. He took me to a movie. I don't remember much about it except that it was about car racing. But I do remember he picked seats in the theatre that were down front and on the side. Watching the movie from that angle made me want to throw up. Afterward we went to Big Boy. I ordered a hamburger assuming we were going to have a complete meal. He ordered a sundae. I felt so nervous and awkward after all those crush years that I couldn't relax enough to even carry on a decent conversation. If there had been a spark, it couldn't have ignited anyway. All my dreams were dashed, and I'm sure he had a terrible time.

After eating, he took me to Hansen's Golf Center to a well-known make-out spot. He gave me the obligatory kiss. And that was it. He drove me home, backing into my driveway, letting me out, and immediately speeding across the street and up into his own driveway. We wrote one more letter, and that was it.

I didn't see him again until his father's funeral. When I got to the funeral, I was a nervous wreck. I immediately turned into that twelve-year-old teenager again, the one with the crush. I couldn't even sign my name in the acknowledgment book. I wondered, *Should I shake his hand or hug him?* I moved my purse, so it wouldn't get in the way of a handshake. When I saw him, we hugged like friends.

"I don't think I've met your wife," I said when I walked up to him and the woman next to him.

"Oh, this is my daughter," he said, setting me straight.

"I'm not saying you look older," and then I dissolved into non-sensical blather, unable to carry on a normal conversation. *Just get out of here before you act any more like an idiot,* I thought to myself as I escaped.

It's amazing how one can revert to childhood so quickly.

* * * * *

Please remember that the following story took place in 1970–1971, just a few years after the civil rights riots in Milwaukee. While working on the Psychiatric Unit at the VA, I met Bob, or Sonny as he was known. Clarice and Art, two nursing assistants, were sitting with me at the door of the unit when we saw him walking down the hall toward us. He was six foot three, black, mustached, and extremely muscular, accentuated by a black T-shirt. Clarice told me he liked me, but I hadn't even noticed him until that night. Following that, Bob and I talked, and one night, we went to the auditorium together. He lifted me up to sit on the stage while he sang to me and played the piano. I was definitely smitten. We dated a couple of times when he'd go out on pass, once to a bar where we ran into one of the nursing assistants from the VA. He promised not to tell anyone, but of course, he spread the word. I probably could have been fired, but fortunately, I wasn't. Another time, we went out with Clarice who was white and Art who was black. They were an older couple and had been dating for some time. After Bob was discharged from the hospital, he moved in with me. It was a one-bedroom apartment, but it seemed large.

On Thanksgiving, I was having dinner at my house and asked my mother how to make something, telling her I was having some friends over for dinner. Being Katherine, she figured out that I wasn't really doing that, and she convinced my dad to drive over to the apartment. They sat across the street until Bob and I walked out of the building. She later called to give me a piece of her mind. Not a pleasant conversation. All of a sudden, our phone began ringing every night at 2:00 a.m. After the first two times, I stopped answering. It stopped for a week, and I learned my mom had gone to Florida on a business trip with my dad. As soon as they returned, the phone calls began again. One night, I answered and said, "Mom, I know it's you, and if you think you're interrupting something, you're not." We never got another call. After a month or so, we found a note on the door, saying, "Did you know you're living with a 'coon'?" Shortly thereafter, the landlord evicted us for "playing music too loud," which we'd never done, of course. I wanted to fight it, but Bob decided we should move, so we found a place across from the VA. It wasn't nearly as nice, but no one seemed to care that we were there. We were happy there, and Bob worked at a home for delinquent boys, while I continued at the VA.

We'd have some of the boys over on weekends and take them on outings. He'd found a bar that wanted him to play his country

Western songs, so he had a date set, and I was really excited. By this time, he had returned to his normal style of dress which was cowboy boots, Western style clothes, and a cowboy hat. All of our friends were going to be at his show, and we planned on having a wonderful night. We waited. We waited. Bob never showed up. He'd gotten such a case of stage fright, that he even asked me to wrap his arm to fake that it was broken. I refused. After that, between his depression and alcohol use, things in our relationship started going downhill. Finally, I agreed to move in with my parents. They came over with the police, fearing for my safety. Bob had broken a table and put a hole in the wall with his fist because he was so angry that I was leaving. My parents continued to call upstairs to be sure I was okay, and I kept telling them to stay downstairs. I truly wasn't afraid for my own safety. Probably the worst thing I ever did in my life was to give in to Bob's request to make love one last time while my frightened parents waited on the street with the police. It's disgusting to me to this day, but at the time, I wasn't in my right mind. I'd grown up in chaos. I was still looking for love, and this is how it all played out. A reason, not an excuse. I then went downstairs, he left, and my parents helped me to move. However, I still managed to see him at the bar we and our friends went to. I'd become very close to a woman named Dale who was also dating a VA patient. I eventually moved in with her. We had a duplex above a bar, and our neighbors raised goats—in the city, on the roof.

They were gypsies! They weren't around too long, and Dale and I lived together for several months. We were at the bar one night—our only source of fun in those days. That night, my dad, at Katherine's request, came in to get us. We went to their house. They lectured us on the sins of drinking, and Dale and I returned to the bar. Dale would become a central figure in my life in later years.

In the middle of all of this, two weeks after I moved out of the apartment with Bob, my dad was returning from a business trip. He suddenly had "waterfalls" in his eyes. It appeared as streams of water in his vision. As the cab driver took him home, he was unable to direct him. He could only tell him "turn right" or "turn left" just as they came to the correct spot. But he had no forward vision of where he was going. The doctor correctly diagnosed him over the phone with a cerebral aneurysm. He was in the hospital for six weeks. During that time, my sweet, soft-spoken father, swore like a sailor. My cousin, Vaughn, and I could only stare openmouthed. When I tried to help him to use the bedside commode, he became very upset at the thought that his daughter would see him in that condition. I told him that, as a nurse, "once you've seen one behind, you've seen them all." He then reluctantly allowed me to assist him. After recovering from surgery, he went home with no residual effects. He also remembered nothing of his time in the hospital. Many people had sent him flowers, and he took pictures of all of them. When they were developed, he looked at them and asked, "Who took these pictures?" He simply had no recall of anything.

After a few months, Bob proposed, and we started driving out to Las Vegas. When we got to Salt Lake City, Utah, we stopped to visit his friend, Smokey Tubbs, and his two wives and multiple children. Interesting situation. We all went out that night to a bar that Bob had sung at in the past. I wondered if he'd really do it this time. As soon as we walked in dressed just like Charlie Pride, everyone immediately started screaming, "Sonny, Sonny!" I sat with Smokey and his friends, and Bob/Sonny actually got up on stage. With the spotlight on him, he announced "I'm dedicating my first song to my new wife, Kathy, and she's right over there," pointing at me. He sang "You Don't Know Me," which was our song. I dissolved in a pool on the floor and never heard the rest of his songs. Upon arriving in Las Vegas, we found a hotel, got our marriage license and bought our wedding rings. Then Bob left the hotel to "do some things for the wedding." He was gone late into the evening, and I was beginning to wonder if I'd be stuck in Vegas on my own without any money. However, when he returned, he gave me some convoluted story, and I assumed he'd just been gambling. We found the Chapel of the Bells where Glenn Campbell had supposedly been married. Our vows were said on August 27, 1971, in front of a minister with two strangers as witnesses. He was dressed in his cowboy clothing, and I was in purple hot pants and white "go-go" boots, popular at that time. Driving home, we had minimal funds and went quite a while without eating. Finally, at a restaurant in Oklahoma, we ran into a couple from Milwaukee. We chatted, they bought us breakfast, and we followed them home, where they let us bunk on the living room floor. It was somewhere on the east side of Milwaukee. People today would never consider inviting strangers into their home, and even then, a biracial couple was not top of the list for many people. We then moved in with a friend of Bob's for a week or two before driving to St. Paul to visit his people. Bob had been raised in sixteen foster homes, and he would sit outside taverns and beg his biological mother to take him home. She always refused. When we arrived, we were greeted by "Ma" a quite large, short woman of mixed nationalities—Scandinavian, black, American, and Indian. The stepfather was dark-black, short, very small frame, wearing a nylon stocking on his head because his hair had been processed. He greeted me with a French kiss, and I quickly backed off, never telling Bob. We had a short visit, and I had my first and last taste of chitterlings. I refused the headcheese, thank you very much. Bob sat on the bed next to me as I called my parents to tell them we were married. Their reaction was, "We don't want to hear about you unless you're dead." I was devastated but not terribly surprised. The night of our one-month anniversary, he took me to meet his foster mother, a sweet, sweet older lady. We also visited his cousin, Kim, black and old enough to be my father, and his wife, Kathy, who was eight years older than I and white. They were delightful people with four adorable children. Bob and I planned to go to California. One day, we were in his mom's kitchen, and he picked me up, spun me around, saying "Kit Kat, always remember, I loved you when I married you, I love you now, and I'll always love you." I was over the moon at such romantic words. He left to get gas, visit his foster mom one last time, etc., but after two hours, I knew he wasn't going to come back for me. I called Kim and Kathy to see if he'd gone there, and they told me that I couldn't live with Ma, so if he wasn't back by 7:00 p.m., I was to call them and stay at their house. When he still didn't arrive, I called Kim to pick me up, and I lived with them for ten weeks. With their family, I felt I'd come home.

Until they died in 2013, on the phone or with our many visits, when I brought all my boyfriends for their approval, I always had that feeling that I was home. During the ten weeks I lived with them, I got a job with Manpower, filing for an insurance company and took the bus downtown every day. In between times found me sitting on the couch, drinking Diet Coke, eating processed boiled ham, smoking heavily, and waiting for the phone to ring. Neither the doorbell nor the phone rang for me. He'd taken my car and my gas card. Eventually we tracked him across Canada and into Southern California, where he stayed. I'd not spoken to my parents since the painful conversation about our marriage, but I decided to return to Milwaukee and start life over. I'd finally admitted defeat. Terry, the friend I'd called during my suicide attempt, was the only person I could think of who might help, so I asked to borrow money to get home. Knowing she couldn't afford it and knowing I'd be upset, she called my parents anyway and told me she'd lend me the money. I found out many years later when my mother was angry with me. "Hmmph! You think you know your friends. Bet you didn't know that Terry borrowed that money from us when Bob left you." Terry said she'd decided to risk our friendship rather than risk my uncertain future. Sometimes you have to do the right thing because it's the right thing. Supposed "betrayals of trust" in the eyes of another are sometimes correct in order to save a friend from the potential greater harm.

Before leaving St. Paul, I went to Rochester, Minnesota, to visit a friend from high school who lived there. While she was at work, a call came through for me. I heard my sister-in-law's voice and was immediately thrilled. We'd found Bob! But she told me to sit down. "Sonny died in a car crash in California this morning." I was quiet. She asked if I'd heard her and repeated the worst words I'd ever heard, "Sonny died in a car crash in California this morning." I was then told I had to keep from crying when I got back to Ma's house because she was so upset. So here's a woman who hadn't cared about her son for most of his life, didn't know where he was for the past eight years, and I, his own wife, wasn't supposed to cry? Sorry. I had to call a college friend, whose dad took me back to St. Paul. Ma's house, a very small upper duplex, was overflowing with family and friends. I got a calling saying Terry and my parents were coming to St. Paul, and I told them to stay in the hotel. My parents would never have survived a situation like that. However, Terry, from a very small town, bravely came to be with me. I was so comforted by her kindness, and I was amazed at the number of people who'd driven up from Milwaukee, friends from the bar we went to, coworkers from the boys' home, Dale, and others. It showed me once again how many people loved us. When his biological father came from New York, I didn't know how to address him. Should it be sir, Mr. Baker, Warren? I'd heard some pretty horrific stories about him. But the minute he walked through the door, I knew I'd call him dad. He stood straight, a dapper, distinguished man, with kind gray eyes. He said quietly, "This must be very hard on you." We stayed in contact until he died in 1980.

Having not seen my husband in several weeks, I insisted on viewing his body. I wanted to be sure I was truly burying the right man. My two sisters-in-law went with me, although the funeral director had strongly suggested we not come. I asked if he could be recognized, and although the answer was yes, he said Bob's face was messed up. Nonetheless, I insisted on seeing him. Each of us had someone from the funeral home behind us in case we "hit the floor." My first thought, when the casket was opened, was "he can't breathe!" as his head was encased in plastic. Bob's accident had taken him over a bridge, falling face first onto the exhaust manifold. When the plastic was removed, I could see one side of his handsome face was very identifiable, and the other was destroyed. It was a very difficult experience, but one I had to go through for my own peace of mind. The funeral director gave me Bob's personal belongings, and my heart was warmed to see that his California driver's license said he was married, and he was wearing his wedding ring. Both were signs to me that at the time of his death, he still thought of himself as married. So I took that to mean he hadn't left me because he didn't love me. Katherine wanted me to come home with them when they left St. Paul because she wanted to protect me from "all these black people." I laughed at that and stayed at Kim and Kathy's for another two weeks before moving back to my parents' house. I'd wake up with nightmares, and my mother would come in to comfort me, saying, "It's okay. You know it's better this way." I was not comforted. At some point, I received a letter from California from a man named Mr. Peeples.

He told me that Bob had lived with him while he was there, and that he'd gone on this journey alone to prove to my dad that he "could take care of his little girl." He'd found a place for us to live and a job and was on his way to send me a telegram that I could come out there. He was suffering from a migraine when he left Mr. Peeples's house, and according to the police report, he didn't see some construction ahead. He passed a truck, tried to avoid the barriers, and went off the bridge, landing on the grass below. Mr. Peeples assured me that Bob loved me very much, and from some of the things he'd included in his letter, I knew Bob had told him to contact me in case something happened to him. That comforted me far more than my mother ever did or could. But once again, Katherine was back in my life.

After Bob died, I stayed with my parents and worked at St. Joseph's Hospital. I worked there for eight years as a staff nurse, a med-surg assistant head nurse and eventually a head nurse in the department. Just as I had in college, I realized that nursing was not the career for me. I enjoyed my peers and interacting with the doctors. Helping the patients was satisfying, but handing out pills and being required to know anatomy and physiology, what the lab results meant, etc. was just not my cup of tea. I told everyone that if I just had a phone, computer, and paperwork in a cubicle somewhere, I'd be a happy camper. But this is the career that had been selected for me, and the one for which I was trained, so what else could I do? Unfortunately, I struggled as a head nurse, finding I couldn't supervise the same people I had previously known as friends. Looking back, I see again that I was depressed, exhibited by always being late to work, not knowing what was happening on the unit, not really caring about things of a broader nature such as committees and allowing my personal life to intrude on my work. My supervisor was understanding and nurturing, but when she retired, I suddenly received a review from the assistant director of nursing. It was negative in every way, and I cried. Asking for help to improve was met with a cold "I don't know what you can do." Much as I hated to give in and give up, I saw this as an opportunity to get out of nursing, so I gave my notice. The physicians were shocked, and many asked if there was anything they could do to help or change my mind. Some of the nurses asked me to stay and were sad to hear that I was leaving. Those things were comforting, but I left nonetheless. Over the next eleven or twelve years, I bounced from one job to the next, nursing home, two psychiatric hospitals, a clinic for weight loss, an insurance company where I didn't even have a phone and got little training. I worked a couple of jobs at a time through Manpower, nursing positions in a floating situation, and even taking door-to-door surveys. I tried very hard to get out of nursing, and I often left jobs without another one to go to, but most of the time, I had to return to it because the others didn't pay enough to sustain me.

While working at St. Joe's, I met a man named Jack. He worked as a bouncer at a bar downtown, the Stone Toad. He was, as usual, tall, educated, well-built with a small paunch, and white, looking a lot like my friend, Jeff. Unbeknownst to me, Jack memorized my name, street address, and the name of the suburb where I lived while checking my ID. He told me he'd call, and I wrote him off as just another flirtation from another guy. However, he ended up remembering only my name and the suburb name. He went back to school at the university in Whitewater. When he returned for the summer, he did a lot of detective work and finally surprised me with a call. I was quite flattered that he'd gone to that amount of work to locate me. He was a romantic, a gentleman, with a good sense of humor and gentle like Bob.

In the interest of full disclosure and attempting to avoid any potential problems in the future, I decided telling him I'd been married to a black man would be a good idea. Unfortunately, I chose to tell him just as we were exiting the freeway. We almost had an accident, but after recovering, Jack seemed to adjust well, but it was actually flag number one. He brought me flowers often. On one occasion, he surprised me with front row tickets to Holiday on Ice.

When we arrived, there was another surprise. A couple we often double dated with was joining us. He was quite romantic. I was totally delighted. The performance was wonderful, and at the end, when the skaters went around the rink for one last time, the lone black male skater crossed the rink to shake my hand. Jack didn't seem to be bothered, but when I told my mother, she was less than pleased. "You must have given him your 'come-hither look,'" she said. I never did know the meaning of that phrase.

Jack and I dated for about six months when he proposed, giving me a beautiful ring. Although I have a great memory for details, and after lengthy review of my relationship with Jack, I am totally unable to recall where or how he proposed. Was it at our special bar, at the lake, at his mom's house, did he get down on one knee? I haven't the slightest idea, nor do I have any idea why I can't remember this rather important event. For the next two months, we'd visit my friend, Terry, and her husband. They came to Milwaukee as well, and once, I think we were even celebrating the engagement. When we went to church, Jack informed me that I could never let his mother know he'd attended a Lutheran church—they were Catholic. Flag number two. Jack also took me to Bloomington, Indiana, Beck Chapel for the wedding of my friend, Jeff, and the love of his life, Joyce. I was honored to be only one of two St. Olaf alums to be invited. I was so happy for Jeff that I sobbed through the entire ceremony.

One evening, Jack and I were watching TV in the den at home, and my mom came in to join us. As she entered, she said, "Well, are you two still engaged," in a tee-hee, cutesy, flirty tone of voice. Neither of us found this amusing. It felt as though we were children playing at being adults.

One night, sitting in the car in the driveway, he said, "If your dad needed to live with us as he gets older, that would be fine. But I couldn't handle your mom." I told him not to worry because I wouldn't even try to put that burden on either of us. Flag number three.

Finally, the flags culminated in another driveway conversation as he was taking me home from a date. He said, "I know I love you. I just can't say it right now." I removed my engagement ring, set it on the dashboard, said, "Call me when you can," and went in the house.

My mother was irate. "Why did you give it back? He would have come to get it, and you could have patched things up." I responded, "Why would I keep a ring from a man who can't say he loves me?" I was really very proud of myself. It felt good to have done the right thing my way. I never heard from him again, and even though he lived in Milwaukee, we never ran into each other. I was sad to lose Jack but not devastated. I had been through the death of a husband I loved. A broken engagement hardly measured up to that.

CHAPTER 5

THE MOST DRAMATIC AND ERRATIC love of my life was Tyrone. Our relationship lasted for roughly nine years. He was black, tall, well-built, not highly educated, but he was definitely street-smart. My friends and I went to the Investment Club, a bar that had live bands or recorded music. This bar became a hangout spot during my time working at St. Joe's forward. We went there, closing the bar almost every night, drinking heavily. Part of it was social; some of it was emotional pain management still handling the death of my mother and Bob and probably even my childhood. We originally went to this bar because the bartender was a friend of Bob's. From day two, the same people who came in became my family. We sat off in our own section, having philosophical, work, and social conversations. It was a bad time in my life, but I look back on them fondly. They were supportive, fun, and caring. This camaraderie was important to me then and is meaningful now.

Generally, these friends were four to six years younger than I. I was a late bloomer, so I fit right in with them. There was Al, Danny, the man who came to my mom's funeral to support me, and Warren. Amber, Jean, and Carolyn were there a lot of the time, and I was never at a loss for someone to talk to.

Carolyn and I bought a drink, and I listened as she shared her latest story about her husband. It was the first or second time we were at this bar. I met Tyrone about three years after Jack and I broke up. One night, with Carolyn and I being the only ones there, the place was dark with the only lights above the bar.

We were sitting at the end of the bar. The bartender came over and said, "The guy at the end of the bar wants to buy you a drink." I looked down the bar, and I couldn't see anyone.

"Tom, I can't see him."

"His name is Tyrone." I accepted the drink having no idea what was to come.

It took him a while to come over, and he introduced himself to us. He got my name and number, but he didn't ask me out until a couple of weeks later. But we did talk as I would sit at a table, and he would talk to us for brief moments. At that point, we started to meet other people, and the group got a little larger when we sat together and talked. But Tyrone wouldn't sit with us because this was a game to him. He would notice me but not speak, or he'd ask me to dance one time per evening, or he'd ask to take me home. It was exciting to me because each time was different. My heart pounded every time he walked into the bar. What would happen tonight?

It was such a weird relationship. I loved him so much, and despite his actions to the contrary, I think he loved me on some level too.

He was more of the chaotic, exciting adventure I needed. I grew up with chaos, and that's what he was. I was also in love with him because he always made me feel special just the way I was. He gave me the type of love I knew too. Even though he made me feel special and did things for/with me that he didn't with others, I was never enough to win out over all the other women. A counselor finally told me that it was okay to keep one tiny part of my heart for him. After that, I never cried again, although I do still remember him at times.

Bob was more romantic, gentle, and kind. There was adventure being with him, because of his actions and our travels. It did not seem as adventurous as the time with Tyrone. He was more of a player. I always thought he was very handsome. When I look back, he wasn't all that gorgeous, but he had a presence, an aura.

I don't know that I ever truly knew him. I knew what he did, and they were not all good things. I got out just in the nick of time, before he ran a large drug business. I learned via the grapevine that he eventually had ten cars, a butler, and a large mansion in Stone Mountain, Georgia. He became very rich. He also spent two lengthy terms in prison, during which his girlfriends and children had little money and had to pool what they had.

I'm quite sure he wasn't doing any mass drug sales when I was with him, but I do think he was trying to get things set up. He protected me from any of the underside of life. At one point, he was looking at opening a bar and did let me in on that.

He lived with a woman and their son and we knew about each other. At the same time, he had another girlfriend with whom he had a daughter.

I have always found that the black people I've met are very down to earth, making you feel loved no matter what. No expectations. You just have to be who you are. He was that way for me.

He always made me feel special when we were together. He would take me out to dinner with his parents. He would take me to the horse track in Chicago. We went for a week of vacation in New York City by way of Canada. One time, in New York, I got angry and walked out at three a.m. In the process I almost got picked up, got cigarettes, came back and he was blissfully asleep.

He wouldn't go sightseeing but in New York City he did drive me by St. Patrick's Cathedral, So, I could see it. I didn't realize it at the time, but in looking back, I think he'd made a drug connection before we left home. I think this because we made one stop while we were there, and I wasn't allowed to go up into the apartment where he was visiting his "cousin." He was only gone a few minutes.

I was his only white girlfriend, and I was the only one he took on vacation. I was the only one to double date with his parents, and he made certain I spent time with his grandmother.

In the beginning, I'd pick him up at American Can, where he worked. We would get something to eat or drink.

The only way I could get in touch with him was to call his mother or "Boo" at a certain gas station. They would find Tyrone, and then he would return my call.

Initially, any intimacy was in his car. After I moved into an apartment in October, he would come over frequently. He would just drop in for a few minutes or a few hours. He pretty much did what he wanted, but I was thrilled at the surprise visit no matter how long it was. At that time, he wasn't working. Sometimes he would stay over. He moved in and out often over the nine or so years.

American Can closed shortly after I met him, and then he didn't work at all for years. He was continually trying to find a way to open a bar or restaurant, anything where he could be his own boss. I finally convinced him to work at a factory across the street. He gave in, worked for a few months, and then decided he needed to be circumcised, just so he didn't have to work for a while. He convinced me to buy a house instead of living in an apartment. I found a home in a poor but quiet neighborhood. It was green shingles with pink trim, ugly, but it was the right size and the right price. We moved in on a hot, humid Fourth of July. He and his friends helped by bringing things in their cars and a trailer. One bedsheet contained his platform shoes and a lampshade. He then left me to get everything settled. I was angry, frustrated, hot, and unhappy.

Tyrone and I never spent as much time together as I wanted to. He would say he would be over or promised to take me somewhere but then didn't show. We talked a lot about marriage, but the true proposal didn't come until later and not for the right reason. Tyrone loved money, Lincoln Mark cars, himself, and me.

One day, I received a call from his mom. "Is your mother dangerous?" "No." I laughed. "Why?" Apparently, there were two white women sitting in their car at the top of the hill where Tyrone's parents lived, and she was a little nervous. I said, "No, they're crazy, but they're not dangerous." I waited a while and called my mom to tell her not to do that again, and she didn't. She said she was trying to find out if I was living with Tyrone, not realizing that Tyrone didn't live there at all.

Katherine was eventually hospitalized for anxiety. The psychiatrist believed her condition was due to my actions and refused to let me visit her. There was no counseling, just Valium, which she eventually stopped taking, using it solely to threaten us with the thought of suicide.

One night, my friend, Grace, her sister, and another friend came to Milwaukee to see a Kenny Rogers concert downtown. Tyrone let us use his black Mark IV Lincoln with a sunroof. My friends came from a small town and had little contact with blacks, and they'd heard a lot about Tyrone, so they were anxious to finally meet him. I asked if they wanted a drink, and they declined. I cracked up when I opened the door of my apartment and watched him walk down the hall. I warned the girls of what was to come. Here was this tall black man wearing a full-length white rabbit fur coat with a matching white rabbit fur hat. Following the short meeting, the girls decided to have a drink, and we had a good laugh. After the concert, which was outstanding, we got into the car. I was trying to back out into traffic in the parking structure, and one of the girls stood up through the sunroof and yelled, "Let us out! I have to get home!" We were in hysterics, but the man behind us was impressed with her performance and let us out. We went to the club and joined my family for laughs and drinks and conversations. All of a sudden, Tyrone walked in. We were all a little tipsy, and one of the girls reached out and stroked his coat. He never spoke to us and never knew of her admiration.

He died in 1999. I never had the chance to say goodbye. I'm big on saying goodbye, but I don't think we ever truly got the chance to say that or formally end our relationship.

To the best of my ability when someone is dying, I get there. However, in this case, I had to read about it in the newspaper. A few years later, I called his stepfather and asked about the last days of his life. I learned that he'd been released from prison to go to his stepfather's house. He could care for him until his death from stomach cancer. Edward read to him from the Bible daily and, at the very end, asked, "Do you believe?" Tyrone's response was, "I do now." After all of his poor life choices, he finally received Christ, and I sobbed.

I was crazy in love with him. It was like an addiction. I couldn't get enough of his energy and his danger.

Tyrone was like the wind. I saw him at least twice a week, sometimes every other day. I would try to drive around and run into him. My mother taught me this strategy. She had begun driving me around to find out where my high school boyfriend was and what he was doing when he wasn't with me. Now I would go out with girlfriends and go looking for whichever man I happened to be dating at the time.

He had an aura about him. He was charming. We functioned on his street smarts. He was intelligent, but we didn't talk philosophy or anything too deep. He had other women. There were many reasons to have me believing that he loved me. One was the fact that I was his only white girlfriend. I was the only one he would take on vacation. He made sure I met his grandmother when she visited from the south. We double dated with his parents.

He took me to see a concert with Isaac Hayes, a famous black singer, who was mainly known for his song from the movie, *Shaft*. As we sat there, the stage suddenly rose from the center of the floor, and there he was, bare-chested, gold chains around his neck, bald head, and sunglasses. All the women swooned, including me. When we came out of the concert, a police car was sitting there. I drove Tyrone's car, but we got pulled over. Tyrone was arrested on his unpaid parking tickets, and I went home alone.

Tyrone also took me to special bars and sometimes sat me up on the bar to show me off. The only night that was off limits was New Years' Eve, when he took out the girlfriend with whom he had a son. It took me a while to figure that out, and I wasn't pleased, except that he always called me just after midnight. He also took me to the horse track in Illinois.

When we needed money, he found a way, but most of the time, I would give him money and supported him. One time, he called me at work and had me leave on my lunch hour to go downtown and bail him out returning in time to finish my shift.

He did what he could to protect me from his world. He saved me from exposure to pot and even more trouble at a party. It was a dark room, and we were all sitting around, talking. All of a sudden, someone handed me a short unfiltered cigarette, and I wondered why. It suddenly dawned on me that it was a joint, and I just passed it on. Tyrone removed me from that situation very quickly.

I did have an abortion early on in our relationship. We were driving down the street and saw a billboard that read "Unwanted baby? Call," and there was a phone number. I'd never seen the sign before or since, but I said, "Well, knowing you, I should probably write down the number," and I did. A month later, I needed it. At that time, it was illegal in Wisconsin, so I had to go to New York. Carolyn went with me. We'd been given instructions to meet someone at the bottom of the escalator in the airport. It was like a grade B spy movie. The clinic was in a rundown office building. Most of the people didn't speak English. I remember hoping that the instruments would be sterilized in between procedures. Tyrone and all my girlfriends knew why I went to New York. I was only gone one day. Afterward, all I could do was eat. I came back home, and all Tyrone asked was, "Did you do it?" Then he took me out to dinner at my insistence.

The timing was challenging. I had just been promoted to head nurse. Mom had gotten out of the hospital after her nervous breakdown. I couldn't think of any other way to handle this situation with everything else going on. Tyrone paid for the procedure. My girlfriends were supportive, but it was Carolyn who went with me and kept me from being a nervous wreck. Per their policy, Carolyn wasn't allowed into the hospital with me, so she walked the streets of New York for several hours. When I was close to leaving, I'd developed a migraine, but no one knew what I was saying. Finally, the doctor came in, and I screamed at him that I had a horrendous headache. He understood enough to order a pain medication. Emotionally, I was so caught up in so many things that I was numb, and I compartmentalized it and never thought about it again, which totally amazes me. It was a baby, and I had the procedure done like I was having my tonsils out. They said, "Do this," and I just did it like a robot.

One night, at the Investment Club, Tyrone, who I had been seeing for five years, didn't talk to me much at all. When Jean and I left the place, we noticed that he had driven his live-in girlfriend's car that night. I reacted instinctively, taking off my platform shoe and breaking both headlights on the car.

Tyrone stopped to see me the next day, asking me if I had done the damage on the car. I refused to admit I did. I let him wonder, letting him think through why seeing another girl's car at the bar might make me angry.

Another time, Jean and I had been out drinking, and we went looking for Tyrone. We went to an afterhours bar he frequented in a poor side of town. I wasn't comfortable about walking in at a late hour in that neighborhood. His car was there, and I noticed that he had left his sunroof open. I climbed into his car through the opening. Someone noticed me doing this and let Tyrone know. He came out just grinning at me.

This next story was wrong at the time and is wrong today. However, it happened, and as you'll hear from Tyrone himself, he was proud of me at that time for doing this. God has obviously changed my heart and mind since then. Tyrone and his friends had been at the Investment Club and told Jean and I to meet them at another bar in a seedy neighborhood. Jean and I parked. We saw Tyrone and his friend walking toward the bar and called to them a couple of times. He ignored us. I knew he was challenging us to walk into the bar alone. I figured I'd recognize him anyway since he was wearing a hat, not even reminding myself that in those days, most black men wore hats. When we did walk in, the place was a tiny hole-in-the-wall kind of place. There was only one other white face in the crowd. I saw Tyrone talking to a woman at the bar. I told his friend, Earl, who had a gold tooth with a dollar sign etched into it, through gritted teeth, "Get him over here!" He tried to calm me down, but I repeated my demand. When he still did nothing, I yelled the N word at the top of my lungs. It became completely, deadly, quiet. Then people must've realized that I was with someone in the bar, and they went back to laughing and talking and drinking.

Jean whispered from the side of her mouth, "What did you just do?"

"I don't know, but I think we should go to the bathroom," which was what we did quickly. We talked about it and couldn't decide if we should come out or not but decided Tyrone and Earl would hopefully protect us. They were waiting at the door when we exited.

We all had a couple of drinks and left when the bar closed. "I can't believe you said that," Tyrone said proudly. "I can't believe my baby just said that."

"Whether it's your turf or my turf, I'm not going to put up with you talking to another woman in front of me."

He never did that again. I'd made my point.

There was one time I was sitting in the Investment Club, talking to Danny, a friend from the bar. We often shared the common loss of our mothers, as well as other things. Tyrone came up and tried to interrupt our conversation. I held up an index finger and asked him to wait a moment.

Tyrone became upset that I wouldn't interrupt my conversation with Danny for him. He picked me up by my neck right out of the chair I was sitting in. The bartender leaped over the bar to break up the altercation. He later told Tyrone that had he not been working, he wouldn't have lifted a finger to help me. For some reason, I was not his favorite person.

The next day, Tyrone stopped at my apartment building. I decided to meet him in the lobby. I didn't want to risk letting him up to my apartment.

"Are you afraid of me?" Tyrone asked, grinning.

"Hell no," I responded.

He actually went to Danny's workplace to tell him to stay away from me. It must be said that although Danny and I had many conversations at the Investment Club, I never dated him outside of the club unless I'd broken up with Tyrone for some period of time. I thought Danny might be a good husband, until one night, he announced he was going to marry another girl who frequented the Investment Club. I wasn't at the bar when he announced this news, and I was devastated when I heard what he'd done partly for my sake and partly because I knew he was definitely marrying the wrong girl. He may have been afraid to announce the marriage when I was there. This marriage only lasted a year.

The way I met Danny was when he sat down next to me one evening, put his arm around me, and said, "Hey, Kathy, how're you doing tonight?" I wondered if I'd had too much to drink at one time because I didn't recall ever meeting this man. He finally admitted that his mom had been dying of cancer on a unit next to mine in the hospital. While he was passing my unit, he saw me and asked for my name. We became instant and good friends. I was also flattered with the way he'd found out who I was just from seeing me at the bar, and the hospital, I have another memory that on July 4, Danny took me for a ride on his motorcycle to go to the lakefront for the fireworks. Every time he accelerated, my head would hit his helmet. Neither of us was pleased with that state of affairs, and we never rode together again. Of course, I also took Danny to meet Kim and Kathy for their evaluation. It was positive.

* * * * *

He was working when I met him. I thought there was hope.

His suggestion to buy the house was a sign to me that perhaps he was ready to settle down, and when he started working again, I was convinced we'd make a life together. After I moved in, he bought me a Doberman pinscher puppy. Snapper ate my couch and my clothes. When he heard a noise at night, he would run to my bed, stand over me, and shake.

I wanted Tyrone to take him away because he was out of control. I finally threatened to take Snapper to the humane society, so Tyrone took him away not telling me where he was going.

One of the memories from this house was a fire that happened there. I was sitting in the living room, talking to a friend on the phone while I was broiling a steak. Suddenly, I saw smoke followed by fire. I hung up and called the fire department.

"I shouldn't have called you," I told the five beefy, strong-looking first responders as I stood there, feeling embarrassed.

"If you hadn't, you would have blown out the whole kitchen."

It was up to me to get the cleanup and remodel done. Tyrone was no help.

Even with the house, which was Tyrone's idea, he was there only twice a week, every other day at the most. He would stop in, stay for a variety of lengths of time, rarely staying overnight.

CHAPTER 6

I'D MET DALE AT THE VA when her husband was on the same unit as my first husband, Bob. She and I lived together for a while, above a bar and next door to gypsies who raised goats. She and I also did a lot of drinking, smoking, and talking. One night, my mom made my dad come to the interns, where we were drinking, and take us home. After they lectured us on the evils of drinking, we returned to the bar.

One day, many years later, Dale called me, and we had a lovely, long conversation. Shortly after we talked, Dale called me back, which was highly unusual. She said, "God has something for me to tell you."

"And what is that?" I asked somewhat skeptically.

"I don't know, but let's talk, and we'll find out."

We talked for a while, and she wanted to pray the Lord's Prayer. In the middle of it, the Holy Spirit made clear to me that I could have a personal relationship with Christ. I was in awe. I called my dad, and when I told him, he said, "That's exactly what you said when you were confirmed." I checked my catechism and found it to be true. Again, I was amazed.

While this was the most important event in my life up to that point, it still didn't totally *"sink in"* until much later.

Whatever faith I had from the past deepened after this, but only a few actions changed. God continued to work in my life and to protect me from myself. But I could only see that much later.

CHAPTER 7

MY THOUGHTS OF LOVE REMAINED deluded and continued to rule my life, including my relationship with Tyrone. Every few months, I'd return to my parents, looking to get the love and approval I'd tried to find since I was a child. When they weren't forthcoming, I'd quickly return to my previous lifestyle. I think I also wanted my parents to learn to like Tyrone through what I told them and see what a good relationship we had. I think even I knew that wouldn't happen and wasn't even true. I also recall a phone call with Christina during which Tyrone walked in with roses. I was thrilled. Her comment was "I'd rather you were with a white man who beats you than a black man who gives you flowers." I asked her to repeat the statement, and when she did, I hung up.

I told Tyrone I could no longer live with him as an unmarried couple, and I moved out. I told him he could stay in the house as long as he kept it up and paid the mortgage. Needless to say, and as you could expect, he did neither. Sadly, I ended up evicting him, which was very difficult for me. We went to court, but didn't speak to each other. He brought a letter that I'd written in passion that he could stay in the house, including the conditions. After testimonies and after reading the letter, the judge said, "I think I see what's going on here" and he threw the case out. It felt like something had been lifted from my shoulders.

My parents again came to my rescue, finding an apartment around the corner from them. It was a lovely place, the kind I'd have chosen for myself as a new Christian beginning my new life. I had fun furnishing the apartment, and it looked so nice. I felt as though I was truly starting over, a whole new life. However, that "new" feeling wore off quickly as you may expect.

As a recently born-again Christian, I decided I couldn't/wouldn't have sex until I got married, and I therefore stopped the birth control pill. Tyrone stopped over to see my new place, and you can guess how long my commitment in this area lasted. The very next day, I called Jean and told her I "knew" I was pregnant. The next step was to take a pregnancy test which, of course, was positive. A visit to the doctor confirmed it, and he gave me a due date of January 18, 1981, my mother's birthday. Out of three hundred sixty-five days in a year, he had to pick that one. I was furious with God. Despite the fact that I'd sinned by sleeping with Tyrone, I felt that God could have stopped the pregnancy. I cried a lot during that period, feeling shame and anger toward myself. I immediately told Tyrone, and he was ecstatic this time. I wasn't so sure.

I'd just been hired at a small clinic and was having all day "morning sickness". I called my soon-to-be boss to let her know what was going on, and she just said, "We love babies. No problem. Just take care of yourself and start when you're ready." One Sunday night, I asked God to please stop the vomiting. "I'm going to lose this job before I even start." The following morning, there was no more vomiting, I drove to work, and never had an episode of sickness again. One of the many miracles God had in store for me.

I then had to decide what I was going to do. Would I have an abortion? I couldn't do that again. But I knew I couldn't keep this baby. It was one thing that Tyrone had abused me emotionally, but I was not going to let him do it to our child. I could just picture him promising him/her and never showing up, saying he'd provide something and not do it, not calling or seeing our child for a lengthy period of time. I just couldn't let that happen. I wrote to my college roommate, and she wrote back, suggesting I think about adoption. I'd never thought of that.

At the same time, I was reading a book called, *Learning to Lean* by Marion Bond West. There were several short stories, and I found one that confirmed God's plan for giving this baby up for adoption. As an aside, I can no longer find that story. In the meantime, I'd gone to a baby shower for a coworker, and while sitting with the group, I felt my daughter's first kick. This was real! I went to a Christian adoption agency, and since I was also filing for bankruptcy at the time, they helped me by saying I could lie and say my piano was actually being held for my father. I thought, *If they'd tell me to lie about that, would they do the same thing during the adoption?* So I decided I needed to go for a private adoption. It was important to me that the couple be Christians. There was a Christian biracial couple, and the wife was a client at my clinic. I was thrilled, convinced that they were the couple I'd asked God to send. I asked her if she and her husband would consider adopting my child, and she said they'd pray on it.

Several weeks later, the day before Thanksgiving, she told me they'd decided against it. I was so disappointed. Jean asked me, "You've only got two more months. What if you can't find someone to adopt her [by this time, I knew it was a girl?]"

"I know God has someone for us, and he'll show me who it is in time."

"Well, what if you deliver and haven't found anyone?" she said.

I responded, "Then I guess I'll keep her and realize I've misunderstood what God wanted." I called a church with an enormous congregation, and I asked one of the pastors if he knew of anyone who might be looking to adopt. He put me in touch with someone who might be able to help, a Christian obstetrician. We talked on a Friday afternoon. The following Monday, she called me with an excited tone in her voice. I started to cry. "I went to a party on Friday night," she said, "and without me saying anything about adoption to anyone, someone came up to me, and they told me Chuck and Sue were looking to adopt. They want to meet you, and Sue wants to call you right away."

"Of course!" I said. I spoke to Sue shortly after, and we set up a time for me to go to their house. I was extremely nervous, but I also felt that this truly was the family.

One evening, a couple of days later, I went to their home. It was beautiful in a suburb of Milwaukee. We talked a while, and I was so impressed and so convinced that they truly were God's choice. I didn't ask many questions at all. They were a white couple and strong Christians. Sue had lost her first husband to viral encephalitis and was caring for three children on her own. She met and dated Chuck, and her children fell in love with him, just as she did. They were married and had two children of their own, one of whom had died of SIDS about one month prior to our meeting. This was early December, and Chuck's grandmother had been praying that they'd have a baby by Christmas, despite being told many times that would be impossible. Grandma's prayers did come true as they had a baby by Christmas, even though she wasn't due until January 18. We talked on the phone frequently, and Sue and I had both thought of the name Jennifer, but Sue had a dream and was given the name Faith Elizabeth. I thought it was awesome. I was seeing a Christian counselor throughout all of my pregnancy because I was struggling with how close to get to the baby who now had a name. Carrying her inside of me of course meant I was close to her. But I was also trying to maintain a distance since I knew I wouldn't be raising her. It was a difficult balance and a daily struggle, especially after she started kicking.

Tyrone was not at all in favor of the adoption and wanted to raise her himself or have his mother raise her. Much as I cared for her, his mother was an alcoholic, so that wasn't an option. He kept asking if he could take her to a small bar to show her off or to the horse track. Obviously, that was a no go, even if I thought he was joking. He wasn't around much, and he certainly didn't help with any of my medical bills or clothing or even doing things for me around the apartment when I was too big to do them for myself. Living around the corner from my dad and aunt, I didn't want them to find out by seeing me walk down the street. So, I went to their house to tell them I was pregnant. They, of course, were very unhappy, and Dad said, "I'm just glad your mother's not here to see this." My aunt said, "Well, we're not going to babysit. I don't normally believe in it, but in this case, why don't you get an abortion?"

"Because I've done that before, and I can't do it again."

"Yes, we know," she said in a nasty tone, "and it was Bob's."

I responded in an equally nasty tone, "No, it wasn't Bob's. You always think you know everything and never bother to find out the facts. It was Tyrone's, and as far as babysitting, trust me, I'd never ask you to come near my child. I just wanted to tell you so you wouldn't find out some other way." As usual, my good intentions were for naught. Many years later, Ruth told me that she and my dad had thought I was telling them that my "clock was ticking" so I'd gotten pregnant, and that's why they "couldn't figure out why I'd opted for adoption." I quickly set her straight and realized again that when I tried to do something nice for them it was always misinterpreted.

I left before things got any worse and almost felt I shouldn't have bothered telling them at all. I kept asking God not to let the birth occur on my mother's birthday, and I was so thankful as that day passed.

Unfortunately, in the midst of all this chaos, I'd made the choice that I needed to file bankruptcy. So, on the nineteenth of January, one day after I was due, I found myself waddling up the steps of the Federal Building. People kept commenting on how big I was, and I just kept on the red coat Ruth had loaned me. Finally, that was over. Or so I thought. The lawyer asked me for the balance of what I owed him. I almost laughed. Here I was filing bankruptcy because I had no money, and he wanted full payment. I reminded him of the monthly arrangements we'd made.

The next day, Danny called me at work. I gave him my number at home, and he promised me he would call. My immediate thought was that I wouldn't have to give up my daughter because Danny was calling to restart our relationship. Instead, he called to tell me that he was thinking about getting married and wanted to run it by me. He told me about his wife-to-be. "Sounds nice," was all I could say. He sounded a bit surprised, and ever since, I've wondered if I'd responded differently, my life would have gone down another path.

A few years ago, his father died, and I sent a sympathy card, including my phone number. We spoke for a while, and he's still married to the same woman. He said, "Maybe we can stay in touch better this time." It sounded good to reunite with an old friend, but I doubt that it'll happen.

The day of delivery, I thought I was having contractions, but having timed them for two hours the week before, only to find out it was just gas, I went back to bed. Pretty soon, the pain was every five to seven minutes, and I called the clinic to have someone take me to work, so I wouldn't have to leave my car there when going to the hospital. They suggested with laughter that I go to the hospital right away. Obviously, being a nurse didn't help me in this situation. A previous coworker, Rita, came to get me, and every time we hit a bump with her little yellow VW bug, I had more pain. She stayed with me all through labor, which I'm told was fairly easy. You couldn't prove it by me, especially when they had to break my water. When I went to the delivery room, there was a point at which I thought, *I think I don't want to do this anymore, let's just stop.* It suddenly dawned on me that this was something I'd have to see through to the end, which came at two thirty-two in the afternoon. Rita has always considered herself an honorary grandmother. Since I was giving her up, the nurses didn't let me hold her, not knowing I had a whole plan in my mind. We stopped at the nursery, and I saw the most beautiful little girl I'd ever seen. I was on a total high and didn't sleep all night. My joy and hormones kept me awake. The supervisor and one of my coworkers came to see us that night, and the supervisor said, "I've always said I'd never have children, but this one makes me think twice." What a lovely thing to say.

As I sent out pictures, I totally expected that people would just "drop-down dead" at her sheer beauty, but no one did, and I was disappointed when my friends told me she was cute. She was obviously so much more than cute. Chuck and Sue asked if they could come to visit, and of course, I had no problem with that. Many people sent flowers and gifts. I will say, when I called Tyrone at work to tell him I was in labor, he did leave to come and get me. He apparently got lost because he didn't show up until the next day. He walked in and saw all the cards, etc., and said, "Oh, I suppose I should've brought you something. Here, do you want this?" And he handed me a chicken leg from KFC. We called for the baby, and I cried. He held her in both hands, kissed her, rubbed noses, and did all the daddy things, saying, "You tell your mommy you're too pretty to give away." All I could do was sob. God gave me the strength to stay with my decision as I tried to show him that this was best for her. He repeatedly asked if I was still going to give her away, and I quietly said yes. He said he'd be back the next day, but after confirming with me that I still intended to go through with the adoption, he never showed up again.

In those days, there were no drive-through deliveries. I would normally have stayed three to four days, but Faith was jaundiced, so she had to stay longer. Since I'd been with her all those nine months, I wasn't about to leave her alone in the hospital. Chuck and Sue were paying for everything, so we agreed that I would pay for my personal length of stay. In order to maintain my sanity and distance, I sometimes fed her myself, and sometimes I let the nurses do it. I totally enjoyed my time with her, feeding her, talking to her, holding her, even changing her diapers. She was so alert, and at one point, she stretched to look around me and see the light from the window. I loved her so much, and I did a lot of crying. One of the aides told me one night, "Are you sure you want to do this? All of us are saying what a good mother you are." It made me feel happy, sad, but not uncertain.

I said, "You don't really understand the situation. I appreciate what you're saying, but this is definitely what's best for her."

When I signed the birth certificate, I spelled her middle name as Elisabeth, using an S instead of the usual Z, putting my own little stamp on her. And so, the day finally came for us to leave the hospital. I had her all dressed in a yellow outfit. The social worker came and swooped her up and went into the hall. I went after her, saying, "Wait, I have to say goodbye. You can't just take her away." I'm sure that's the way they had to do things with teenagers, but I was a thirty-three-year-old woman giving up the only child she'd probably ever have, and I had a plan. So they waited for me, so I could hold her, say my good-byes, and give her a final kiss.

Faith had to go to a foster home for a time, until Chuck and Sue could be licensed. Suddenly, it dawned on me that I'd never be a real mommy at home with my child. I called my counselor and asked if it'd be okay for me to bring Faith home for a day. He was hesitant but agreed. He called Chuck and Sue to warn them that I might change my mind. I knew I wouldn't. I just needed this day, and it was special. I borrowed a car seat and went to the foster mom's house and felt the same love I'd felt in the hospital. We came home to my apartment, and the first thing I did was to cut off a lock of hair to keep for myself. I fed her and changed her diapers, but mostly we sat in the rocking chair and talked. She actually turned her head to watch the soap operas with me, and she gurgled when I talked.

I'd let Tyrone know the day before that I was going to have her if he wanted to come, and he said he would. Of course, he never did. However, my cousin, Vaughn came and spent a few hours with us, mainly so he could take some pictures. She cried when I gave her to him to hold which made me feel as though she'd already made a connection with me. Funny the things you think about and hold on to when you know time is short. At the end of our special day, I drove her back to the foster home, sobbing all the way. I gave her to the woman after kissing her one last time, returned the car seat, and sobbed all the way home. I'd enjoyed that day immensely, but I still knew I was doing the right thing.

Tyrone wanted to meet Chuck and Sue before he'd sign the papers, so we went to his house, the one I'd bought for us. I was embarrassed, knowing the house they lived in and the poor little thing he lived in. But they didn't seem to mind. He asked questions about why they wanted to adopt his little girl, and many times when Sue would answer, I'd think, "Oh, don't say that" or "that's the wrong thing to say." Tyrone finally agreed to signing, and then after telling Chuck, "Your wife is a fox", they left.

He said, "Take good care of my little girl."

Surprisingly, Tyrone wanted to take me out for lunch, and we had an actual conversation, the first in a very long time. Most of the things I had worried about Sue saying were the exact things that had impressed Tyrone. There was God again, knowing more than I did. But why was I surprised? He always did. One of the judges had a problem with a biracial child being adopted by a white family, so a social worker had to make several visits to Chuck and Sue's house to be sure this was the right place for her. The social worker was totally impressed with the whole situation, and she had no problem recommending the adoption.

Chuck and Sue got signatures from their neighbors stating that they'd be more than happy to accept a biracial child among them. The final decision was made with all of us sitting around a conference table at the courthouse. Present were the judge, the social worker, Sue, Chuck, and me. The judge asked me what I thought. I responded, "They are a Christian family, and they are the couple I want to have Faith." The social worker and the adoptive parents talked about why they were in, and the support their neighbors had voiced. The judge made the adoption final at that meeting.

It was also agreed upon that I could bring Faith to their house instead of just handing her over in a cold courtroom. We were elated.

I didn't hear much from Tyrone after that, although on occasion, he'd call in the middle of the night. Sometimes it was just to talk and tell me he loved me, sometimes it was to tell me I'd made the wrong decision, and once it was to tell me, "You're just a bad mother." I answered, "A mother's job is to give her child the best life she can, and that's what I've done." The calls and visits went on for a couple of years, until one night, I was at a late season pro baseball game with a girlfriend, and it was boring.

"I feel like getting into trouble," I said to Cathy.

We drove to the bar, the afterhours place that Tyrone owned. We pulled up just as he was walking over to escort another woman into the bar, but when he saw me, he left her and came to me. Needless to say, it made me feel good, just like it always did. We went in with him, and he was his old self, glad to see me, ignoring everyone but me, and putting on his sexy personality. We talked for a while, and then we had what would become our last dance. It was a slow dance, and we wrapped our arms around each other, and it was just like we were the only ones in the room. My heart was exploding, and yet I somehow knew this would be our last time together. And it was.

My nine years with Tyrone were strong, negative, addictive years that came with many lessons. I learned not to live my life solely on heart and emotions. God taught me also to use my mind and my gut instincts in the face of strong emotions. I learned that if I listened, God would tell me what to do and even orchestrate the whole process for me. Placing my daughter was the hardest thing I've ever had to do, and when Tyrone did all the daddy things in the hospital, God still gave me the strength to do what I knew he'd planned for this child.

On my first Mother's Day after Faith's adoption, I found myself kneeling on the blue carpet in my apartment, totally drunk, telling myself, "I can't do this. I should never have given her up." I begged God to bring her back. In that moment, I felt God's presence surrounding me with a spiritual hug, confirming I had done the right thing. Of course I still cried when I told this beautiful story, but I never again cried out of pain.

Sue would send photos and notes every so often. Then they stopped. I wondered why. It turned out she thought it would hurt me more to get photos. I would take the photos to work and tell my coworkers, "This is my daughter." When I'd look at her photos, I thank God for letting me have a little part of her life. I was astounded to be a part of someone so special. She's athletic and tenderhearted. She got the best and worst parts of her father and mother.

When Faith was ten months old, Chuck and Sue invited me to their home, and Faith crawled all around the living room, stopping at each person. When she got to me, she put her arms up for me to pick her up. I was so touched; I cried. Then at age two, they again invited me to see her. I said no because at that age, they have developed little personalities, and if she had said no and hidden behind her mother, it would have crushed me.

Sue suggested that when Faith turned eighteen, it might be the right time for us to meet, but Faith was not ready at that time. Nonetheless, we met briefly in Chicago, and it was awkward. She showed me her scrapbook detailing her activities when she was younger. There was still some awkward tension while we ate dinner, and Chancy and I left soon after.

We really had no contact after that. Sue and I stayed in touch.

Faith and I started to e-mail a little bit when she was in college. She was still not ready. I understood she was probably angry. She had a right to be. She denied that she was.

Sue and I had several phone conversations updating me on Faith's life. At one point in time, Faith was struggling.

I cried to Sue, "Are you ever sorry you took her?"

"No, she is our daughter," Sue exclaimed. "And we love her."

I felt guilty Faith was putting them through so much.

When Faith's daughter, Ariana Grace, was born, Faith let us come up to the hospital to visit them shortly after the birth. We took a picture of the three of us, and I felt bonded with something so special. Chancy and I each got a minute to hold Ariana, and of course, we took pictures of that too. When Ari was about two years old, Faith asked if I would come for two days to watch her after Faith had had surgery. I was delighted.

Faith and I talked about the election. She had never voted. "Really?" I reacted. She felt judged. "I'm just surprised," I said. "I never knew anyone who didn't vote." We had a long argument. I got in my car and left, but I decided I had to go back and leave on good terms. She wouldn't talk.

About a year ago, out of the blue, she called, and we started talking. She brought Ari after Christmas. She didn't recognize me with my hair longer. I gave Faith a gift card and Ari an ornament, just as I do for all my grandchildren. It was an enjoyable and comfortable two-hour visit.

Faith wanted me to tell her about the adoption from beginning to end. She requested this on a Saturday but said she wasn't ready to hear the story. Could I do it on Monday? She'd heard parts of the story from various people and now wanted me to tell the complete version from my perspective. She called me the following Monday, and I told her the whole story. The only time she cried was when I told her about leaving her in the crib.

I've become Faith's older friend. She's resolved her anger for the most part, and it seems we can discuss almost anything. I enjoy her calls, although I've had to limit them to an hour, because I can't handle more than that with anyone.

CHAPTER 8

M Y SUPPORT TEAM HAS BECOME dearer and more valued to
me as the years go by.

My oldest friend is Grace. She's from a very small
town, and we met when we were fourteen at Pine Lake Lutheran
Camp. We happened to be assigned to the same cabin. Otherwise we
didn't have much in common. She was athletic. I wasn't. Her faith
was strong at that time. My faith wasn't. As we continued writing,
our relationship got deeper. She was one of four cabin mates. After
our camp week was over, we wrote. Grace and I more than the others.
Her family would come up for State Fair, and we would catch up
when they were in town. She told me later that she always thought I
had the perfect family, the perfect house. She later learned the truth
as I filled her in on my crazy family life. Grace loved my dad. She
had a crazy mom and a lovely dad too. We connected on our family
history.

Our lives took similar paths until 1969.

I surprised her showing up for her wedding. Vaughn drove me
to her town.

I always thought Grace had a perfect family and marriage, but
as with me, I later learned that wasn't the case. They divorced seven
years ago. Evidently, he laid hands on her. He earned the paycheck,
and she did everything else. They had one child, Lee, and adopted
a second, Tasha, for whom I was godmother. In addition to being a
wife and mother, she worked as a bookkeeper for many years. When
her husband retired from the railroad, they had several businesses.
Grace always kept the books. Since the divorce, her ex has had so
much animosity that he does not attend events, even those involving
their children.

74

In their marriage, they lived in nice homes and took nice vacations. They lived in Germany while he was in the service. He cheated on her there while she was pregnant. She came home until he ended his tour.

They had their first child, who was the love of both of their lives. Her son was close to his mom. Following the divorce, their son continued to work for his dad and maintained loyalty to his dad in order to keep his job, but when he could, he reestablished his relationship with his mom.

Grace now lives with her son and his family. Unfortunately, Tasha got into drugs and, at forty-three, is still using. She maintains sporadic contact, but her daughters from an unsuccessful marriage still visit Grace.

One time, Grace's husband came up on a business trip and took Jean and me out for dinner. We were enchanted with him. He talked and listened to us. He was very charming. I had a crush on him and avoided visiting them for an entire year, until I got over him.

I called to tell her I was married the day she delivered her son. She was horrified that I had married Bob. However, just before Bob died, she was a big help when I didn't even realize it. I'd asked to borrow money so I could get home from St. Paul. She didn't have it, so she went to my parents to ask for money to help me. Many years later, in an argument, my mother said sarcastically, "Yeah, you think your friends are so loyal. You don't even know what Grace did a long time ago." She, of course, wouldn't tell me what had happened, so I called Grace. She hesitantly told me that she'd borrowed the money from my parents. "I knew you needed to get away from where you were, and I decided that, even if it broke up our friendship, I had to get the money. Your parents were the only ones I could think of." How could I be angry? And how could Katherine not see that friendship sometimes means risking everything for the greater good.

Two days later, I learned that Bob was dead. Grace drove up with my parents, terrified of the neighborhood and the family. I told her not to come to the funeral. I didn't want to put her through that. Bob's dad met her during her visit and flirted with her which made her uncomfortable. They stayed two days. She was already married with two children, and she left those responsibilities to be with me.

I put Grace through so much when I was dating Tyrone. She would call every Sunday, and I would go on and on and on about him. She would give advice, but mostly she listened while I sobbed and blubbered about whatever was going on at the time.

Several years ago, Grace was diagnosed with ovarian cancer. It was my turn to be supportive. We both used "Market Day," and I would send gift certificates. I would call daily and go down to visit every now and then.

Having beaten the cancer, she now works as a home health aide, covering three clients a day. She's had to work since the divorce, sometimes holding down up to three jobs to make ends meet. She has lots of supportive friends in her small town. She has an amazing faith. She's always positive saying things like, "This bad thing may have happened to me, but God is still supporting me."

Another friend I had for a long time is Jean. She'd been like a sister for twenty-seven years. She was the unit clerk when I was a head nurse. We lived close, attended the wedding of a friend together, went out for a drink afterwards, and after that, we just clicked.

She had a wonderful father and an alcoholic mother with mental health issues. She was the oldest with three younger brothers. From the moment, we grew closer until twelve years ago, every adventure or mundane thing we did together was fun. We'd go out, go home, and immediately get on the phone and keep talking. We did everything together. She was a petite, cute, bespectacled, funny, caring person.

She went with me when I visited Kim and Kathy in St. Paul. She'd go with me to visit Grace. We drank every night at the Investment Club and had our own group of friends with whom we shared conversation and fun. She dated Tyrone's brother, Darryl, for about a month. We shopped together and had silly laughing fits.

We went to the movies. Even when I was dating, we would still do things together. She was just the best friend. She was a good mother to her three children, and I was godmother to her daughter.

She was amazingly caring. I shared more with her than with anyone else.

She would tell me I had many personalities, saying, "Oh, I think that's personality number fifty-six coming out." We'd just laugh. We shared everything.

Jean married an alcoholic, partially because she was pregnant. I was so against this marriage I didn't attend. She was the typical enabler for her husband. In response, she attempted to control everything going on in the family. She had to be the strong one.

Jean finally achieved her lifelong dream, going back to school to get an associate's degree, bachelor's, master's and work as a cancer nurse. She worked in hospice, chemo wards, a variety of jobs available in the cancer treatment field. She was extremely successful, and I always admired her.

She finally divorced her husband when she was working on her bachelor's degree. His family backed him and was actively mean to her.

I don't know the catalyst, but about twelve years ago, I guess I did something that offended her. It was something I said on her daughter's birthday. We were shopping, and her daughter was whining.

"Maybe we won't bring her with us next time," I suggested, jokingly.

This comment supposedly ended our friendship.

After a couple of months of her acting differently than she ever had, I asked over the phone, "What's going on?"

"You don't want to know," she replied. Well, of course, then I really wanted to know. She finally told me about my comment and added that while we were in a small store, I had just walked out.

I said, "Well, I was done, so I walked out to the railing to just watch the people while I waited." People watching was one of the activities we'd shared in our friendship.

I realized it had to be a deeper issue, so I tried frequently, sometimes daily, to discover that issue. I got nowhere. She'd dodge my questions or give some vague answer. We exchanged e-mails and letters, sometimes heated, for about two years.

Finally, in frustration and sadness, "Let's go out to the Country Inn, get dinner, stay overnight, and work through this problem," I suggested. We went.

We spent the evening together. The next morning at breakfast, I said, "Well, you still haven't told me the problem."

She said, "Well, we were having so much fun." So I still didn't get an answer.

We continued writing letters and e-mails with me trying to get at the issue. She could write long letters, ten pages at a crack. The letters would say nothing that cleared things up for me. Instead, she criticized me, ignored the sisterhood we'd shared and generally confused me more than before.

I would take it to my friends at work. They couldn't see where I had gone wrong. We went back and forth on it for two years.

"Stop fretting about this. She's nuts."

"But she's been a friend for so many years."

I came home one day. A wall plaque I had given her was hanging on my door. It contained a note, "It's been hanging over my bed, and I couldn't stand looking at it anymore." I wrote to her, saying, "I think you're being a bit passive-aggressive here. When I find things that no longer have any meaning, I just throw them away."

Sometimes with friendships, you must handle changes. Life changes are inevitable.

Jean and I were like sisters. When either of us took a different path, we brought the other along and taught the other the new things in our lives. But when friendships end, you are sometimes left to deal with the changes yourself. You have to accept the end of a relationship.

Her daughter married and invited me to the wedding. There was little conversation between Jean and me. The friendship fizzled. The letters between us were less frequent. She told me that both grandsons were divorcing their wives because they were too controlling.

"Like their mother," I quipped.

"I had to be controlling," she wrote angrily.

Of course, I already knew that—I'd been through it all with her, and I was amazed that she felt she even had to say that. I decided that was the end, and I never contacted her again.

Suddenly, six or so years following this experience, we received a Christmas card from her, signed, "Fondly, Jean." The next year, another card signed, "Warmly, Jean." After that, there was no contact. Our onetime sisterhood was irrevocably finished.

It leaves me sad because I can't really fight what I don't know.

Another important friend is Harper.

I met Harper when she was dating Tyrone's brother, Darryl. He was extremely abusive. She dated him for a year and got out of the relationship. She and I had a lot of drunken adventures as it turned out she was an alcoholic, and I was drinking heavily. One night, we went to a Holiday Inn Express downtown where the Milwaukee Brewers went to party. I was dancing with one of the more well-known players when his wife walked in, and we quickly separated.

She was another of my successful and most unique friends.

Harper was a home economics teacher. She then did an internship for Ford as a third-party mediator in customer service. They created the same position for her in Detroit. She worked for them for twenty years.

She was interested in historic preservation. She bought an old house and fixed it up herself, a true DIY.

She was married twice. On her third husband now and this marriage has lasted twenty years, so I think it's working. She had alcoholic parents and was an alcoholic herself. She was adventurous which was often related to drinking. We would do double dates. We went to the Riverside Theatre to see the movie, *Superfly*. We laughed but thought that the guys were picking up tips to start a drug business. We thought they were silly and that if those were their plans, we certainly weren't going to be a part of it.

She moved to Chicago during her current marriage, working for a company that did historic preservation. Her job was scouting for buildings that could be preserved and then fighting for status.

Recently she changed jobs. Instead of locating buildings, she works for a firm in Madison that gathers funding for nonprofits. She does a lot of traveling for that job. Recently, she and her husband bought a condo in Chicago and have completely renovated it from painting to walls, to furniture, to a new kitchen. I've only seen pictures, but it's totally beautiful and completely her style.

I've known her for forty-six years although sadly, we don't communicate as frequently as we once did.

I've been blessed. I have been friends with Grace for fifty-eight years, Jean for twenty-seven years, and Harper for forty-six years.

I befriended Carolyn when she moved and enrolled at my high school. She says I was the only person to pay attention to her. We met in choir and became friends. In high school, our outside activity was shopping at Mayfair back when the ice rink was still there. We never skated. We would walk, shop, and have lunch. We drank a lot, just as I did with Jean and Amber, and we smoked cigarettes and talked endlessly.

Her parents lived in a wealthy section of the city thanks to her grandmother, who paid for their lifestyle, even though it was by no means lavish. Her father sold carpeting. Her mother worked as a salesperson. She was a lovely lady, very gracious.

Carolyn was dating a boy from her old high school. We talked about him a lot. He was not the kindest person. Shortly after he graduated from college, they got married. His father was a pastor. She worked at a golf course. Carolyn didn't complete college, but she was never without employment.

She and I spent a lot of time at her house when we were in high school. We didn't like to spend time at my house until I moved to an apartment. She didn't have a car, and I did, so I would come to her. I felt comfortable there. She had two brothers and a younger sister.

Carolyn and her husband divorced due to his cheating and general inattention before having any children. Their marriage lasted three years, following seven years of fighting, arguing, and cheating while they were dating.

Shortly after her divorce, she was with me the night I met Tyrone, and after many "one-month stands," she met Mark, her current husband. She and Mark were an instant relationship. They came together fast within a year after the divorce. They met at a pool setting, and for many reasons, she decided to take him under her wing. She learned as they went along that he was intelligent and funny and just an all-around good guy. Mark was in IT. Her first husband was a pretty boy. Mark traveled extensively to places like Japan and Thailand. Carolyn would go along and would write me when she was away. She made friends wherever they lived, and they finally settled in Texas.

She loved weaving and had a full-scale loom to pursue this hobby.

In their travels and through their social life in Texas, Carolyn and Mark gathered a group of international friends. She gets them together at least once a year. Carolyn travels all the time. One of her favorite trips is to visit her sister, Wendy, in Maine who is a pastor.

Carolyn lost one of her brothers to death five or six years ago.

After her father died, her mother remarried a wealthy man who treated her well. When her mother died, Carolyn went out west to take care of her stepfather. After he died, he left his estate to her in thanks for her care.

Carolyn loves interior decorating.

She contributed to the comfort in which she lives now with Mark. They've lived in several houses, one of which they had built. She has thoroughly enjoyed making each of them a home with its own personality. With him, she had two sons who have given her grandchildren.

She stayed in touch, even though she was in Texas.

She is into numerology. She did a humongous chart for me. It made sense while she explained it to me.

They used to come up to visit Mark's mom when she was alive. The last time they were here, we went out to lunch. Our conversation volleyed between numerology versus Christianity. Neither changed the other's mind.

"It's hard to get rid of me," she would tell me.

We've been friends since high school, fifty-four years. Carolyn is in good health, but Mark still struggles. When she travels, he slips and drinks too much. She doesn't do anything about it. She doesn't rock the boat.

He very rarely travels with her.

But he is lost without her. He gets to find out how much she means to him. He warmly welcomes her back from her travels.

CHAPTER 9

I HAD ALWAYS WANTED TO parachute from a plane. When I was thirty-five, I gave that experience to myself. Ruth made sure to let me know that if I broke my leg, she and my dad would not take care of me. On a bright sunny day, I took myself to East Troy. In the morning, the class received a lecture about how we should fall, and then we practiced our landings off a high platform. I aced the test and went off to sit under a huge tree to have lunch. Vaughn came out to take pictures and as it turned out to give me support. I put on the twenty-five to thirty-five pounds of equipment and fear took over. I told Vaughn I wasn't sure I could do this.

"I'm not telling you what to do," he said. "But you've always wanted to do this. Do you want to go home having done it or spend the rest of your life regretting not doing it?"

I thought, *You know, he's right. I guess I ought to do it.*

I climbed into the plane with four other people and the pilot. As it became my turn, the spotter asked if I was okay. I said I was terrified. He told me it was normal to be scared. I said, "No, I'm terrified." What I hadn't heard him tell us was when we sat in the doorway, our legs would be pushed by the air rushing by up against the plane. As soon as I got out on the platform and reached for the strut under the wing and I stood up, my training kicked in. I inched my way to the end of the platform, counted to three, jumped, and flung my arms back as we were taught, and the parachute opened. I looked up to see the red-colored chute and did a 360-degree turn to check out my surroundings. The instructor was connected to me by walky-talky, and he let Vaughn talk to me too. The instructor told me to kick my feet if I was having a good time. It felt like I was only up there a minute, but Vaughn told me the instructor left me up there longer. It actually was about five minutes.

As I got closer to the ground, the instructor told me to flare which meant to take the grips and push them down to your hips, and this was hard. I managed to land in a cornfield, and my landing did not have a major impact, and it felt like I landed in cotton. By then, the jumpsuit had gotten really hot not to mention picking up and folding the parachute, and I got even hotter. In the end, I enjoyed it all, except the work of putting this away afterward. Nonetheless, I accomplished my dream, and I got to experience another feeling of freedom.

CHAPTER 10

A FTER TYRONE, THERE WAS A married man, a patient from the clinic, who pursued me. During his appointments at the clinic, I enjoyed talking to him. One day, I was talking to this man about getting my oil changed. When I left work, I found a note on my car in which he offered to do the oil change. I agreed he could.

Because this man was married, I could see the problems in this attraction, but as always, I went full steam ahead anyway. I was still looking for that person who would love me for who I was. My coworkers strangely were pulling for me that something good might happen for me.

At first, he seemed like a perfect answer. The dalliance with the client met a need romantically, filling the emptiness of Tyrone leaving my life.

This man restored my pride, ended my hopelessness, and I quickly fell totally in love with this awesome man. In that sense, though morally wrong, the client restored me to me again.

I was just sitting there in my apartment, and I noticed a guy riding by on his bicycle. It looked like my client. Since he changed my oil, he knew where I lived. The next day at work, I asked if the man had been him, and he quietly told me it was. That night, my girlfriend and I sat under a big tree at a church near my apartment. When he rode by, I called out to him. He circled around and stopped. My girlfriend suddenly had to leave.

He and I walked back to my apartment. He wanted to use my bathroom, but I just couldn't let him see my chaotic place. I told him I'd planned to go to my dad's house around the corner, and being chivalrous, he walked with me. I went up the steps at the back door, intending to stand there until he left the corner. Unfortunately, when

I peeked around the house, he was still there, so I had to go inside. I told my father what had happened. Dad and I spied out from behind the curtains. He finally left, and although it was late, Dad got dressed and walked me home.

After that, he came over every night. Mostly we stayed in. Sometimes we went for rides around town. Now and then, we went to the movies, risking seeing *ET* at a theatre near his in-laws' house. I could talk to him about anything. It was the most romantic relationship. He had a key to my apartment, so while I worked second shift, he would stop over, and he'd be there, having drawn me a bath, and lighting candles for when I got home. We would go for long walks, and one night, we saw the aurora borealis. He bought me heart earrings for our one-month anniversary. Once, he brought his son over when he did my oil change. He was adorable. We played soldiers while his dad worked on the car.

Another time, we went to the Menomonee River Parkway, watched the ducks, and he asked me to tell him my pregnancy story. He actually teared up, and that was very endearing to me.

Labor Day weekend, he went up north with a couple of his friends to decide what he was going to do about his marriage and me. When he got back, he came over. I sat on his lap, and he told me he couldn't divorce his wife. We both cried. I said goodnight to him, walking him to the apartment building door. After I closed it, I stood there as he got in his car. I could hear him sobbing. To this day, I still run into him around town in stores, restaurants, and we talk.

It was a therapeutic relationship for me, returning to me all the emotions and traits that Tyrone had taken away.

Shortly after, I left the clinic and desperately tried to get out of nursing. I worked doing door-to-door surveys. I worked for an insurance company, doing virtually nothing, for all of about two weeks. I worked as a float nurse for a service. I did all kinds of jobs, but nothing worked out.

I always ended up in the hospital or working in a nursing home.

My client friend would go out drinking and would end up visiting me mid-shift. I thought the drama was wonderful.

The night guard at the nursing home always teased me about getting me a date with Brewers' legend, Pete Vuckovich. One night, he invited me and all of my fellow nurses into the lounge near the front door. None of the windows had curtains. Suddenly a man walked in with a Vuckovich jersey on. He started to strip. Eventually, he jumped on my chair. I should have pushed him away. When it was over, we all walked away silently back to the job. I actually went to the director of nursing to tell her what had happened, but he was never disciplined. It was embarrassing for me and for my colleagues. I worked there for three years.

CHAPTER 11

NEXT, I WORKED FOR A medical hospital that was switching over to a psychiatric facility. For a while, we had just a couple of medical patients in the whole hospital, then none at all. I went to management and kept questioning. "I need to support myself. Are you sure this is actually going to make it?" Eventually they filled two floors of the place with psychiatric patients.

I enjoyed that work. I would sit on the floor and talk to the patients. One time, I experienced a patient moving from one personality to another. She became a little girl right in front of me. One of the psychologists observed my work with the patients and said, "Y'know, you really should be a psychologist." I called my dad to tell him. I was so excited and flattered.

"Uh, uh, uh, don't get a big head," he warned me. Another put down, and it hurt more coming from my dad. I hung up.

One day, the director of nursing called the staff in for a meeting. She asked if anyone thought one of the staff was prejudiced. No one did. On the way out, I said to one of my friends, "Well, at least that can't be pinned on me." We laughed, as the director called me to her office. I said, "You've got to be kidding!" She told me she couldn't believe it either, but the black medical director wanted me fired because I'd shown prejudice in three situations with his patients. It turned out that I wasn't working when two of the incidents happened, and in the third, the patient was being cared for by another nurse. Later, as I saw the doctor walking out, I asked if I could speak with him. We went to a conference room, and I told him the story from my perspective. I then told him my husband was black, and that my first husband was also black and had died.

"Did you kill him?"

I was stunned but went on for reasons unknown to show him a picture of my daughter. We talked a few minutes, and I got up and left. I was furious with myself for not standing up to him and for letting him get away with what he'd done and said.

I'd always gone by the name, Kathy, but it was during this period of time that I decided to change my name to Kate. I felt I was changing into a strong, clearheaded woman, and I needed a name to go with that. Thinking of Katherine Hepburn, whom they called Kate, I decided that would be a good choice. It was a difficult change for some, and to this day, there are only a few people I still allow to call me Kathy. Just for information, a name doesn't change a person, and I hadn't made the changes as fast as I thought I had.

CHAPTER 12

I WAS LOOKING AT THE newspaper one day and saw that there were a lot of want ads for the VA hospital, but there were no psych positions listed. Something moved me to call them. Turns out, they actually had psych nursing positions. They interviewed me and hired me in May of 1987.

In June, Chancy was admitted to the VA with PTSD and depression. He had threatened to kill someone. I never paid attention to him since he wasn't assigned to my caseload.

I was sitting outside a room doing a one-on-one with another patient and heard Chancy telling his aunt on the phone that he was going to lie to get out of treatment. As he walked by me I said, "It's a shame you made the call in front of me."

"Why?"

"I have to report you."

From then on, there was a sort of flirtation going on between us. He always wore his sunglasses, and that was against the rules. So I'd only give him his medications if he took them off, and then he'd put them right back on and sit where I would be able to see him. On the fourth of July, he asked me out. I told him I didn't date patients. He told me later that my comment hurt him.

Eventually, I gave him my number.

During this time, my dad was diagnosed with Alzheimer's disease. It was, as is usually the case, a slow-progressing disease. I would visit him, and he'd know who I was, but then I'd watch as he buttered his napkin, thinking it was bread. I felt very sad. He came to my apartment one day to see if he could fix a plumbing problem I'd been having. When we went into the basement, he looked around, and he started to cry. "All these years I've helped everyone else, and now I can't even help my daughter." I assured him it was not a problem, but I knew just what a frustrating problem it was for him. He was in the stage where he knew he had Alzheimer's, but he couldn't always figure things out, and he knew that too. During this period, he did have the presence of mind and desire to make a beautiful photo album for me with pictures from the days when he and my mom dated through to my graduation from college. I treasure that to this day.

Ruth needed my help one day because she wasn't feeling well. I went to the house, and my dad was too confused to figure out how to let me inside. We finally managed to help him open a window. I got the key and got in. I was able to help her, and she was totally amazed (all I did was give her a few sips of Coke because her blood pressure was down a little, and she was dizzy). In the end, she decided to give me a key to the house in case something happened again. I continued to visit, but I never needed to use the key. During every visit, she'd hover around us, making sure she could hear any and everything we said. She'd always bring up something negative from my past, and I would spend the next few days crazy and upset with her and our relationship. The last straw was when she asked me to return her house key. For some reason, having a key to someone's home, being trusted in that way, was extremely important to me. I exploded. Assuming that my dad wouldn't know if I visited or not (by this time, he didn't always know me) and feeling I couldn't take any more of her similarity to Katherine (I'd come too far from that point, and she was pushing all the old buttons), I never visited again.

Finally, I learned she'd had to place my dad in a nursing home. I called my cousin, Vaughn, and asked if it'd be okay for me to visit. He told me it would, and I went the next day. My dad knew me at first but then became confused. He thought that he, Vaughn, and I were opening an auto body shop, and that I was supposed to put up the signs that day. I tried to reorient him, but he pounded his fist on the table, saying, "You never finish anything!"

I assured him I'd put up the signs on my way home. I was back again two days later, and he didn't know who I was no matter what I said. It made my heart sad to see him in that condition. People are correct when they say that Alzheimer's is like a death and almost harder on the family than on the person him/herself.

While all this was going on, Vern, another patient, was getting out but didn't have a place to stay. I let him stay with me because he had a girlfriend, who lived with her parents. We used to lay out in the sun in the backyard of the apartment building, and friends would come over to talk. It was fun, and I had the best tan I'd ever had. I was so naive, that I had no idea he was growing pot plants in my apartment, and that he and his girlfriend were smoking pot while I was at work. When I learned what I should've already known, I told him he had to leave.

Vern went to the VA and told my supervisor that he was living with me, and that I gave him Valium. I admitted he was staying with me, but absolutely denied the Valium story.

On my fortieth birthday, Jean, my friend, Jim, and his girlfriend were over to help me celebrate when Chancy called. We talked, and I met his cousin over the phone. I suddenly realized that my car was in the backyard. Vern was in it, drunk, and we couldn't rouse him. We called the police. The police discovered that he had an open warrant for his arrest. They took him to jail. It was quite the fortieth birthday.

One day, Chancy came to the VA to visit me. He came up on the unit and stood in the middle of the hall with people walking all around us. He pointed his finger at me, and he said, "I'm going to marry you."

"I don't think so. I'm not even going to date you," I replied.

"Wanna bet?"

"Yes."

We shook on it. Chancy had been a patient in the psych ward at the VA for PTSD (he'd threatened to kill a man for disrespecting his mother), and I'd already had a tough experience dating a patient. Besides, Chancy was not my type. He had a Jheri curl down to his shoulders, very thin, and not classically handsome. However, I had to admit there was some chemistry between us, and he was cute on some level.

Chancy was in the Army from 1969 to 1971 and did a one-year tour in Vietnam. Just before he was deployed while in boot camp, he was sent home to see his mother who was dying of breast cancer. She was only forty-six. He had to return to the army after her funeral. He was one of fifteen children. One of his sisters died of pneumonia when she was just eighteen. Chancy had seen a good bit of hard times seeing family members die. His oldest sister took the younger ones in, including the deceased eighteen-year old's child. She raised them all and her own four children, plus adopting another child much later in life after fostering him for several years.

The only thing Chancy told me about Vietnam was the time he was out in the field on a night so dark he couldn't see where he was going. All of a sudden, he heard a very loud deep roar. He took the sound as a sign from God to get out of the fight. He told his commanding officer he had to go. He, of course, said no. Chancy said he held his rifle to the officer's mouth. There is nothing in his service record of this incident, but he did spend six months in the stockade for "failure to report for duty." He tells the story to anybody who will listen, and he tells it the same way every time. When discharged, it was under an "other than honorable" declaration. This has since been upgraded.

He has a 100 percent disability. It was extremely difficult to get through the red tape proving his disability. After I heard Reagan's Veterans' Day speech, I wrote him to seek his disability pay. I was so angered; I just had to write to tell him to "put his money where his mouth was." Over a year was spent trying to resolve this problem and suddenly two weeks after my letter, when Chancy talked to his veteran's affairs contact, he found out his 100 percent disability had been approved.

Chancy was very poor at the beginning of our relationship, living in a duplex. He wouldn't even let me see. He had to borrow money to take me to the drive-in for our first date to see *Crocodile Dundee*. The date went fine. We shared our first kiss. He claims it was my idea. I claim it was his.

Afterward, I asked him if he wanted to come in.

"If I come in, I'm staying the night," he said.

"If that's the case, I'm taking you home."

Within a month, he moved in. He was living in a very tough place. I would see him at his aunt's bar after my second-shift job for a couple of drinks, and I'd go home. He would walk me to the car to make sure I was safe.

He started talking to me about getting married. I was not pushing, but he continued to bring it up. We eventually set a date for a year after we met on his grandmother's birthday. I was planning the wedding with members of his family when he suddenly stopped talking about getting married.

He was using marijuana and alcohol at this point in his life. I got frustrated and wrote to all the proposed bridesmaids and grooms-men to tell them the wedding was off for now.

We spent a lot of time going out with his family or going to his aunt's bar. He would upset me by staying out with his cousins (although I had no idea who he was with), sometimes all night doing drugs. I cried a lot. A couple of times, I called Sam, one of his brothers, to cry on his shoulder and ask what I should do. He was usually somewhat consoling and encouraged me to be patient.

Chancy would talk about wanting to be with me to his cousins but complained to them that I wanted him to settle down. His family agreed he should settle down. These conversations were going on unbeknownst to me.

Chancy would get hairbrained ideas. At one point, he wanted to buy a fixer-upper-type house where the ceilings were leaking, and the toilets and sinks were overflowing. He had two children from a previous marriage. They were about twelve and thirteen years old.

Once the house was ready, he wanted to bring them home to the fixer-upper. All I knew there was no way I was going to raise those kids, having given up my own and knowing nothing about how to deal with teenagers.

Two weeks after my letter to Reagan, he got his back payment from the VA now that his PTSD was considered a disability. It was a substantial sum. He paid me back for the expenses I had paid for since I'd known him, and then he bought expensive gifts for relatives. The rest, quite a lot, he spent on drugs, and by that time, he'd gone to cocaine. But I wasn't aware of that. I just knew he never had money anymore and was home even less.

All of this took place in the summer of 1988, but a few months earlier, my dad was taken from the nursing home to the ICU. He was dying of pneumonia, a common complication of Alzheimer's. Vaughn had called me, and it ended with Aunt Ruth, Vaughn, and I being the only ones there for his last moments. I was able to have short minutes with him, and I still recall his white wavy hair and his clear blue eyes, looking up at me. God gave me the gift of allowing Ben to know me, and we were able to say, "I love you." He started to ask, "Then why didn't you ever—never mind," which I assume would've ended with *visit me*. I wish I'd had the opportunity to answer. As I'd visit, I'd say, "It's okay, Daddy, you don't have to fight anymore. We'll be fine, and Jesus is waiting for you." I said it three different times after they'd turned off the medication, keeping his blood pressure up, and each time, his pressure went down, until he finally fell asleep. It was peaceful. He was *home* and completely without care, so there were few tears from us. Ruth had a small memorial service. We buried him, and we had very minimal contact after that. She did call to check on me but was very put off when Chancy answered the phone. He hadn't been doing that before just because I didn't want any surprises for my family, but by that time, I thought it would be okay. As usual, my best efforts weren't enough.

CHAPTER 13

CHANCY AND I GOT AN invitation to look at a time share. Doing this in the middle of the week meant we would get some pretty good gifts such as a barbeque grill and a stay at their sister resort in a lovely city in Panama City, Florida. We went, and when Chancy looked at their brochure for the property, he said, "Looks like a good place for a honeymoon." I was shocked! "Is that a proposal?" He said it was, and it finally came out that he was terrified of standing up in front of everyone we would have invited to the wedding. So that's the reason for his previous sudden silence on the subject. Eloping was fine with him. Considering racial issues at the time, particularly in the south, I wasn't sure anyone would marry us, a biracial couple, in Florida.

I wrote to a Baptist pastor, asking if he would, and he said it wouldn't be an issue.

I bought a light-blue bridesmaid dress. His cousin tailored it and did the flowers and a floral headpiece. In the middle of all this, I decided to get the little things taken care of like having a mammogram. When the radiologist, whom I knew, walked in, I said, "Oh shit," knowing they'd found something. I immediately got on the phone to tell Jean, my best friend.

Later, I calmly told Chancy, knowing he'd freak out if I was upset. He said, "I'll be here for you." I saw a surgeon the next day, and a biopsy was done. When I saw him again to confirm the results, I said, "You can't be serious. I'm getting married in two weeks." Sure enough, I had a tiny but cancerous lump in my right breast. Five pathologists had looked at the tissue. While three thought it was malignant, two thought it wasn't. They sent the sample to a pathologist in Kansas who dealt only with breast tissue. His finding was that it was a malignancy. The doctor gave me the choice, and I said, "I couldn't live with the doubt." A lumpectomy was done, also checking the lymph nodes under my arm. Fortunately, the nodes were negative, but it was a harrowing experience nonetheless. I was in the hospital for two days, and Chancy was a visitor for about fifteen minutes on one of those days, which really made me feel very lonely. The oncologist said it was the type of cancer that required only radiation therapy, not chemo, which was a relief. I had daily treatments, five days a week, for six weeks. Chancy didn't quite know how to handle things and didn't go with me.

Since the process only took about fifteen minutes, there really wasn't any need for him to go. I never cried. I just put one foot in front of the other and did whatever they told me to do. We barely even talked about the cancer, choosing instead to concentrate on the wedding.

On the day of the last radiation treatment, I came home, sat on our bed in a peaceful blue room, and I cried the entire rest of the day. Surprisingly, a few months later, Aunt Ruth called because she'd heard I had cancer and wanted to know how I was doing. I was touched by her concern.

We decided to go on with the wedding. Once at our destination, we went to get our wedding license, but it was Columbus Day, and the government office was closed. It turned out the Baptist Church couldn't do our wedding because it was under construction. So he found a beautiful spot on the sixteenth floor, the roof, of a hotel. It overlooked the beach and the gulf, and it was an absolutely gorgeous day with blues skies and a slight warm breeze. The minister arranged for a justice of the peace and a police officer to marry us. One was black, and the other was white, which was rather ironic. The hotel staff stood up for us and took pictures.

We went to a restaurant we knew and had a wedding dinner which the restaurant gave us for free. We took a walk along the beach. There were reeds and other great foliage waving in the warm breeze. We took photos of each other. We went back to the condo which was beautiful, two stories, a soft pastel coral paint on the walls. We asked a guy to take a photo of Chancy carrying me over the threshold.

"Hurry up. I can't hold her any longer," Chancy said, through gritted teeth. I only weighed five pounds more than he did that day!

He took pictures of me throwing the bouquet and showing the garter, all of the usual wedding things.

Unfortunately, due to fatigue and Chancy's pot use, there wasn't a wedding night.

Three months later, we were still arguing about pot, drinking, and settling down. He decided to visit his kids in California. Unknown to me, he had thoughts of getting back with his ex. I wanted to go with him. He wouldn't let me. He said he would stop to say goodbye before he left. He didn't.

Chancy took a female cousin with him to California, which really upset me when I found out. She told me later that all he did was talk about how much he loved me despite my insistence that he settle down. The first call he made to me from the coast, he told me he wanted a divorce. The second call he made he said he wanted to settle down and make our marriage work. The next call was from his cousin. I'd left the VA and gone back to work at the small psych hospital. I'd been made director of nursing on a Friday, and on Saturday, I was working second shift. I was finishing up my work late that night, and I got the call saying, "Chancy's dying. You have to get out here right away."

I dropped everything, borrowed money from a coworker, and threw a bag together as I prayed over and over, "God, please don't let it happen again," remembering the death of my first husband in California years earlier.

I didn't cry. I didn't have time, just the need to get there and see for myself what had happened. His symptoms had begun the day before he was to start the long ride home. Complaining of a headache in the back of his head, Chancy got home from bowling, got out of the car, started vomiting, and passed out. By the time I got there, he was in the hospital. Fortunately, he went to a trauma center. He got a diagnosis of a massive brain hemorrhage due to cocaine use. Evidently, he was having nose bleeds, his cousin reported, on the way to California.

It was a difficult trip for me. Chancy was dying, I was meeting his ex and their children for the first time. Carolyn, his ex-wife and her husband met me at the airport and walked in with me to the ICU. As I turned and saw him, my knees buckled. They had to hold me to get me back to my feet. He was laying in the fetal position; tubes were everywhere. One was even coming from his head. They had to open his skull to ease the pressure from his brain swelling.

When I would go up to the bed, he got agitated. As I walked away, he would be fine. Something told me to tell him, "I love you, and I always will. I'll stay with you, and we'll go through this together." After he heard all that, he calmed down. He told me years later that he'd been afraid I would leave him. He was relieved hearing that I would stay.

His brothers all drove out in a van to see him because he was dying. Many of them, I'd never met. With that and meeting his kids and ex-wife for the first time, it was extremely stressful for me. I worried that since she was the one who'd gone to the hospital with him, and since his brothers were there and since Chancy and I had only been married for eight months, I wouldn't be the emergency contact.

"What is your last name?" one of his brother's asked.

"Clark."

"Then you're his wife."

The social worker understood my concerns in that area and was very supportive. The nurses and the family were worried about me because I was either in his room or downstairs, talking to a friend on the phone. They wanted me to eat and take care of myself. At one point, I was having a cigarette outside with one of his younger brothers. We were just standing there quietly when I suddenly said, "I really need a hug. Could you give me one?" He did. I must have really needed it because I wasn't in the habit of asking for a hug from anyone much less a virtual stranger.

The doctor predicted that Chancy would die or would spend the rest of his life in a nursing home. But there were a lot of people, several hospitals, and much time and hard work ahead.

His ex's husband had suspected that Chancy was coming out to take his wife away from him.

"I hope he dies," he said as we sat in his living room. I should have slapped him, but I was so shell-shocked by the whole experience that I never said a word. Part of Chancy's family from Decatur, especially his oldest sister, just knew he was going to be fine. She didn't come out with the brothers but stayed home and prayed. Some of his sisters wondered if we were really married. They were ready to criticize, and perhaps step in if, they didn't like my decisions. The Decatur part of the family was ever watchful.

I shared with the cousin who traveled to California with him that Chancy got agitated when I made my visits. She turned around and told his aunt in Milwaukee that the nurses reported that he would get agitated when I visited. But no nurses were present when he got agitated, and the cousin was the only one I told. It was clear who filled in his aunt.

I realized when he was still in his coma that I would need a job if he died or if he lived. This assessment moved me to go home. Leaving him was a major stressor. I went home which was controversial, which I understood.

His sister, Marvell, came out and stayed with him after I left. She wasn't working at the time. He was still in the coma when I left. I called twice a day. One day, when I called, his nurse was excited.

"He's awake and talking." They had been concerned to see what functions remained. They reported that he was making sense to his nurse and responded to her requests appropriately. It was a huge moment for us.

Next day, I called and talked to his brother, Curtis. He put Chancy on the phone.

"Do you know who this is?"

"My wife."

"Do you remember my name?"

"Of course, it's Shirley." Shirley was the name of an old girlfriend.

"Do you want to try again?" I asked.

I flew out for two days for my birthday. By then, he was out of the ICU. He was very coherent.

I gave him a bath, and he got a little "touchy-feely" with me.

"I hope you aren't this way with the nurses."

He giggled.

I continued to call the nurses and do my job as the director of nursing. I spent a lot of time on the phone with my friends and my pastor helping me keep it together. He was only able to get into a chair. We talked a lot, and he did his best to keep up his end of the conversation.

I've been trying to establish a timeline of this chapter of my life. Six weeks into his ailment, he was moved to the VA in California. Those weeks felt like a year. Marvell stayed with him when he moved.

He was going to come to the VA in Milwaukee. Marvell left for home as I arrived in California. They met me at the airport. It was the first time I met her. She was a tiny pretty lady with hands quite crippled by arthritis. She didn't let that affect her. She now has a master's in education and had started working on a PhD. She got very frustrated with me when I kept having to change my plans on coming to pick him up.

I was able to bring him to the VA in Milwaukee. It was six weeks after my birthday. I was worried he wouldn't remember me. I walked into the room, a six-bed ward. The minute he saw me, he had a big grin on his face.

"I didn't know if you were going to come."

The nurses said he had bitten one of them as they were putting in a catheter. They had to put one on for him to travel.

"If you bite one of the nurses again, I will come in and put your catheter in myself."

He behaved this time.

I spent the night in a conference room nearby with my clothes I planned to wear the next day carefully folded for the wake-up call in the morning.

His son came to get us to the airport. We did a wheelchair transfer. Chancy helped. His son stayed until our flight was called. The flight attendant helped get him and his urine bag on the plane. He slept all the way home.

When we got home, I got him into the car myself. I left him in his wheelchair as I went to the parking lot. He sat still waiting for me to bring around the car. Someone was kind enough to sit with him.

I got him transferred into the Bronco even though the seats in that car sit higher. He helped the best he could. We drove directly to the VA, I got him out of the car into the wheelchair, and he said he had to go to the bathroom.

I got him in the hospital and found a men's room. As I pushed him in, I announced a woman was in the men's room. It took me a bit to get his trousers and underwear off and arrange his catheter so it was out of the way. He proceeded to tell me he didn't have to go. I could have hung him.

Admission and registration complete, someone came down from his floor and took over.

I was exhausted. A couple of days later, a couple of his relatives called, threatening to kill me because I hadn't let them know as soon as I'd gotten him home. I was sincerely afraid and called Chancy's oldest sister. His dad happened to be there, and he kindly called the relative, saying, "She's the boy's wife. Leave her alone." I was so grateful, and I never was threatened again. We eventually established a relationship.

When I came back the next day, he was almost comatose. I literally slapped him in the face to wake him up. His nurse walked in.

"I have his pills."

"What are you giving him?" I asked alarmed.

"Valium."

I was very upset.

They had not used his California records. They were using his Milwaukee medical history.

"I want to talk to the doctor."

I was told he wasn't on duty that night. He called me later at home. I was livid. I got them to change everything. But I wondered how other vets did without an advocate.

They transferred him to the rehab floor. Even in this department, I was upset most of the time. The care was not good. They told me he wouldn't eat. He couldn't cut his meat. He couldn't help himself. He would have a wet bed. After he was in clean, dry clothes, and sheets, he ate just fine.

They let me take him home on weekends. He loved meatloaf TV dinners. We would also go out for dinner. He would do fine. We finished our meal one night in a restaurant.

"Are you ready to go?" I asked him.

"Yes."

He didn't move a muscle. He just didn't move. I paid the bill and left. I thought if I walked out, he would follow.

He didn't.

I asked the hostess if she would tell him they needed the booth.

"It's not our policy."

Frustrated, I went back to him again.

"Are you ready to leave?" I asked him, trying hard not to go shrill.

"Yes," he said. He got up and left.

It was infuriating and funny all at the same time.

His family came up to see him at the Milwaukee VA from Illinois. I had told him they were coming. I got him set in his chair, putting him in a posey, so he wouldn't fall out of his chair. I went to get his family from the lobby. By the time, they got to his room, all he had on was the Posey. He got all his clothes off, sitting there grinning.

I had Chancy home one weekend, and when we got to the VA Sunday evening, he surprised me.

I got out of the driver's seat and came around to help him out of the car to go back up to his unit. As I got to his side of the car, he used the power lock button in his door to lock me out. He refused to unlock the car. He didn't want to go back into the hospital. I begged and pleaded with him. Finally, I called up to his unit, looking for help. For a while, they didn't send anyone. Then one orderly came down. He couldn't talk him into unlocking the car. He told me he wanted to go back home. I was almost resigned to driving him home. Then a second orderly came down. On the way home, I said through gritted teeth, "You know why I'm mad, don't you?" And he replied, "'Cuz I wouldn't go back to the hospital." I informed him that he would be returning the following day, and he did.

After much physical therapy at the VA, he was not able to walk without assistance, and he couldn't dress himself on the weekends. I would always listen carefully for the sound of him opening one of the doors of our home. I was afraid, fueled by stubbornness and adrenaline. He would walk out, which would have been dangerous opening him to further injury. His doctors were going to discharge him, and his social worker commented to me, "We don't have any more hope for him." They were sending him home with no follow-up care as they supposedly couldn't find a Medicare authorized facility that would take him.

I began to look around for another facility that could continue to work with Chancy. I don't remember how I found the rehab facility that he needed. I'm convinced it was the Lord's doing. I found a small rehab facility, Visitors Hospital in Buchanan, Michigan. I drove him to Michigan to settle him there. They had a good, ample staff who would give him great care and turned out to be terrifically effective. Medicare paid for this therapy. I made all of the plans to admit him.

They evaluated him, and he met their criteria.

I drove to Michigan every weekend to see him, leaving home early Saturday morning and returning late Sunday night. They had a house on the grounds where loved ones could stay when visiting. One time, when I was there in the middle of winter, there was a terrible snowstorm, stranding me. The lights went out. I was alone in a house where I was unfamiliar, in the middle of a field of corn, and I was a little scared. I called my girlfriend, carefully dialing with shaking fingers, to tell her what was happening. We laughed at my predicament, and I began to feel better.

One time when I was there, we left his room to go to the cafeteria. He just took off down the stairwell, ignoring the elevator. I thought he was going to kill himself. To my amazement, he had no problem whatsoever. I was completely astounded by his progress in their care.

After six weeks in Buchanan, he was mobile, able to feed himself, dress himself, and able to come home. Every now and then, he still had issues with self-care such as gargling with his cologne. He insisted on putting his shorts over his pants. His brain would get stuck, and he'd insist he was right, so I'd have to let it go for a while. He definitely had memory problems along with the cognitive ones, but all in all, he was doing excellently.

On the day I brought him home and was going to get him settled in his house, I was requested to meet on a busy city freeway with three of his sisters and two brothers-in-law. They wanted to visit and see how he was doing. I was certain they were there to inspect me and our relationship and home situation. I eventually realized that they were just being protective. Here was this little white girl, married only eight months, taking care of him far away from them and hearing stories about me from others. They didn't know what to think and felt the correct need to check things out for themselves. Once again, I was surprised by a call from Ruth who had heard about Chancy's condition.

When I brought him home for good, he began therapy at Curative, an excellent, free-standing, outpatient rehab center. Every morning, before I went to work, his cousin, Elvoy, would come to stay with him until the transport bus came to pick him up for the day. He would be there all day until the transport brought him home. On the weekends, he'd go to work with me. The hospital was going through certification, meaning my staff and I had to rewrite all the policies and procedures. Being the control freak I am, I felt I had to review my staff's work, so I ended up doing the work myself. Chancy was, in general, patient with being at the hospital with me for the Saturdays and Sundays, but he wasn't pleased. Their normal period of treatment was for one year, but he stayed with them for five years because he continued to improve.

One day, early on, he decided he didn't want to go there any-more. I panicked, and I called the administrator, Terry Young. On the next morning, a Saturday, Terry met us at Curative and talked with him, having him sign a contract stating he would attend the center daily. It worked. They had him doing all kinds of activities, physical therapy, speech therapy, occupational therapy, outings. We'd have activities to practice at home. They taught him to ride the city bus on his own, even changing routes. When they felt he was able, they found a volunteer job for him at a nursing home. He did a variety of transport tasks, taking residents to and from appointments and helping to take them on outings. He continues, twenty-six years later, to transfer patients to appointments within the facility three days a week for two and a half hours. He loves this job, and everybody knows him around Wauwatosa.

Another interesting moment at this point came when he got the mistaken impression that I had bought a life insurance policy and had plans to kill him to collect the payout. He shared this impression with his psychologist, Terry. He talked about killing me with one of the knives in the kitchen before I could kill him. Terry told me to hide the knives at home as a precaution. Terry gave me his home and cell phone numbers, just in case.

At the same time, Terry asked him if he trusted me to take him to the VA for a checkup, and he responded that he did. I took him to the VA, and the doctor, who spoke no English, insisted on seeing him alone. Within a few minutes, he came to get me—neither of them could understand the other. After reviewing his case, he told me that Chancy had a brain injury.

"No, it's his PTSD." The doctor and I went back and forth right in front of Chancy. He ordered a CAT scan. After sitting in the waiting room for an hour, I said, "Do you need this?"

"No," he replied.

"Let's get out of here," I said, and we did.

There have been bumps in the road since.

He's also been diagnosed with paranoid schizophrenia, which—combined with his PTSD—can cause some unpleasant behavior.

We'll plan where to go, even be packed and going with people we know, and he'll suddenly decide he's not going. No amount of cajoling, discussing, screaming will change his mind, and I know "the voice" when I hear it. A few years after our trips to Israel and Greece, we were leaving for South Africa, insurance bought, suitcases packed, leaving in two days. Then from him, the voice. We didn't go. He's taken appropriate meds ever since. But even so now and then, I have to get him to take an extra tablet because he's gone off on a tangent, where he'll perseverate on something negative and explode in anger over it. Normally, Chancy loves to travel, and we've taken numerous trips around the country both by air and by car. I've had to do all the driving as he's no longer able to drive because of his cognitive deficits. Being like my dad in that way, I've never minded, and we're great traveling partners, wanting to see everything there is to see, ready to stop at the same times, and enjoying the scenery along the way.

I went to a conference in Rhode Island with my friend, Kathy, for a week. Chancy was convinced we were having an affair. When he gets an idea like this in his head, it doesn't go away, and to this day, he occasionally brings it up. Just a couple of years ago, he suddenly raged at her, saying she couldn't store her car in our garage. The misinterpretation had once again reared its ugly head in his mind. I had him take some additional medication, and he was fine and very apologetic to both of us.

While he was making progress, his sister, Marvell, would call every single day, usually just as I was getting home from work. She would make every suggestion available as to what I should be doing to help Chancy. It used to drive me crazy. However, in talking with her recently, I learned that the reason she was so overly protective of her older brother was because she was operating on the information being fed to her by another family member. The family thought it was coming from me. Once she learned the truth, she stopped calling as often, and we became friends.

Curative taught him to do dishes and laundry. He picked up these chores for me and does them to this day. He says it gives him a feeling of purpose.

Curative also taught him how to ride the bus and placed him at the Lutheran Home, a facility for the elderly and those receiving rehabilitation, as a volunteer. They were somewhat reluctant initially because they'd had a disabled volunteer in the past who ended up requiring more assistance than the residents. Chancy is still there, three mornings per week, twenty-eight years later. The residents love his caring, compassionate personality, and he's able to use his talents. It gives him a purpose, and he enjoys it.

CHAPTER 14

I LEFT THE PSYCH HOSPITAL with little notice when I felt the system was no longer one I could work in. As was my pattern, I had no job to go to, but I applied to several companies at which I could use my medical knowledge without actually practicing it. In the meantime, Chancy and I decided to drive to Washington, DC. We had a wonderful time seeing all the usual sights and taking the underground transportation, which was an interesting challenge. While there, I got notice that I'd gotten three offers of work. To me, it wasn't a big deal. I thought that if you had a degree in nursing and could walk and breathe, you could get a job. However, looking back at some of those I'd interviewed as director of nursing, I realized it really was quite flattering. So on a payphone, I accepted a position at Primecare when I was in my forties. My initial job was in utilization review, where I went from hospital to hospital every day to determine if it was medically necessary for our insured to remain hospitalized. At some points, I traveled to five hospitals in one day, which was exhausting. In one way, it was good, in that I could stop at home to check on Chancy and provide him with assistance if needed.

After about a year, I moved into Precertification, where I worked with Kathy, with whom I now share a long-lasting friendship. Providers would call if a surgery seemed to be needed or equipment was required to support an insured person's health. We would look at our criteria, confer with our medical director who was a physician if we needed more information, and we would let the provider know if the insured would be covered. Kathy and I had a unique relationship. We're both stubborn and need to be right, so we'd often argue (which used to drive some of our coworkers crazy), but then, at eleven thirty, we'd go for lunch.

I loved this job. I finally had my desk, computer, phone, and a window facing the outside.

Our CEO decided to build a brand-new building for our company in the nearby Research Park. Kathy and I would drive over on our lunch hour to the new office as it was being built, taking photos, excited about how construction was proceeding.

It was around that time that we were bought out by United Healthcare. Larry Rambo, the Primecare CEO, was so wonderful to work with. He made it a practice to meet each employee during their first week and get to know a little bit about them. He never forgot a name. Larry continued with the merged company until the atmosphere changed becoming less employee and customer oriented. Larry eventually left the company and started his own. He ended up in Kentucky at some point.

While I worked there, we moved around the city a lot. For a while as we waited for Primecare's new building to be finished, our workforce was divided between three locations. After a year, we finally moved into the new building together. The move was pretty smooth. We moved our own department. Kathy and I sat close or next to each other until the last year of my employment. We moved around the building a lot, frequently sitting in different spaces, but we remained together because we worked well together. However, there was one period of time that we didn't speak at all. She had misinterpreted my tone when talking to someone else and thought I was being derogatory against her. Instead of telling me, she just stopped talking. I was usually the one to make up when we had a disagreement, but after learning why she wasn't talking to me, I decided to reverse the roles.

Shortly thereafter, we were asked to help out at the AARP insurance building on the other side of town. We were still not speaking. However, one day, we faced the infamous 9/11 attacks. People began pulling TVs out of their desk drawers like crazy, which totally amazed us. We made a little small talk regarding the horror we were watching, but I then went back to not conversing with her. Eventually, she called me at home and asked if we could talk. "About what?" I responded, and she later told me she thought we'd lost our friendship. We did talk, and she said, "But it's always been your role to make up." And I agreed, saying, "I'm not doing that anymore. We have to talk things out." And thankfully, that's the way it's been ever since.

My role eventually changed again, and I was then doing claims, auditing, monitoring that the correct payments had been made, and recovering lost dollars. At one point, several people suggested that I apply for a lead position, and I applied. Prior to my interview, I realized something about me and my career. I was always good at my job, so I was promoted until I reached my highest level of incompetence (Peter Principle). I told the interviewer of my decision, she respected it, and the interview ended. I eventually moved on to contract auditing, and so did Kathy. We were trained, but when we got our first printout, we had absolutely no idea what was printed on it, and looked at each other in disbelief and confusion. But I must have known something because my first case saved the company $600,000.00! I just knew I'd done it wrong because who gets that kind of result on the first try when they don't know what they're doing? But no, in fact, I'd done it correctly and was delighted with a small bonus.

CHAPTER 15

Kathy is a fun-loving, creative, knowledgeable LPN. We share a love for the Brewers and Packers, and we both love to eat. She's one of four children with whom she is very close, and she's included us into her family for many years. Her heart is big and generous, and she loves to volunteer her help no matter what's going on. You will see her heart and her eagerness to help later on in the book.

She should have been a party planner. She planned all the parties in the office, and they were a huge success. Today, after retirement, she creates amazingly decorated desserts—cupcakes, cakes, etc. The designs are intricate and colorful and tasty to boot. She's now gone on to experimenting with other delicious meals, and we've spent the past Thanksgiving and Christmas with her and her brother.

One party she planned was my fiftieth birthday party. I will never forget that day. I had always wanted to take a limo ride. The only problem was that I'd planned a small pizza party, and although I was inviting ten to fifteen coworkers and family, I ended up inviting pretty much all the people on my floor and then some.

The party took place on a workday. One sister department sent flowers. Kathy had baked a cake with tombstones on it. I received gifts of Depends, laxatives, and other items supporting old age. Too bad, I didn't keep them.

"I have to go out front. Come on, let's go." I went with her and sitting there was a limo. The moment still reaches me and brings emotion even as I tell the story years later. I looked back at the building, and people were standing in the windows and on the lawn, laughing and applauding. I'm hard to surprise, but she and they did it beyond imagination.

As the driver took me to my house to get Chancy, I started to work through the four little bottles of Asti in the back seat with me. She'd even provided something nonalcoholic for him. We headed for the lakefront, and I asked the driver if I could stand up in the open sunroof. He pulled over, and I stuck my head out and pulled over a jogger.

"Today is my fiftieth birthday, and my friends got me a limo," I told her, grinning from ear to ear. She wished me a happy birthday, laughed, and went on her way. We went to Mama Mia's for the pizza party and were again greeted by a sea of people. By that time, I'd had all four bottles of Asti. That night, though I had given up smoking long ago, I had just one. I thought it was appropriate to have one, and that was that. I was too drunk to stop myself. Chancy feared I'd start smoking again, but I never did.

It was so much fun, and it was a day I'll never forget. Kathy, you'll learn, is the kind of friend I truly needed all along, and especially in these latter ones.

So far, I've spoken only of Kathy, but I developed many friendships among my coworkers, most of which ended when I left or gradually diminished. Some of us still get together on occasion, and no time seems to have passed, although we don't stay in touch in between. There are, however, two others with whom I have continued friendships and who are very special to me.

One woman, Lynn, I thought didn't like me when we first met. It turned out she didn't even know I existed! When she finally became aware of my presence, we began a friendship that has continued until today. We've had many adventures, and we can laugh over the silliest things, playing off each other, long enough that our sides and faces hurt. We are both diehard Packer fans, and one day, we were watching a game on TV, screaming loudly. The window was open, and the little girl across the street called out, "Why are you two yelling?" We closed the window, laughed, and continued to yell. Lynn is a very sensitive, warmhearted woman with enormous empathy for others. She is the most informed, intelligent nurse I've ever known, and she's constantly updating and researching her medical information. She is a quietly thoughtful, generous person, who does many things without letting anyone know. She lives at Hallmark card stores. She brings belly laughs and silliness to the relationship, which are the fruit of friendships, necessary for a healthy life. It reduces stress. It is another way of bonding. Friends allow me to cry. Lynn, will hear me out about the situation that upsets me, and then she'll cry about my problems even when I am not. You can't beat that kind of empathy.

Chancy and I spent a week with her visiting New York City, seeing all the sites. New Yorkers told us a destination was just a few walking minutes away, and we learned that New Yorkers have no idea how long it takes to walk three miles. We enjoyed some plays on Broadway and other more touristy locations.

We frequently enjoy the productions at the Fireside Theater, a dinner theater about an hour away.

She understands Chancy's communication style and easily enables him to be a part of our conversations.

We enjoyed another trip to New York this year to see the musical about Cher and celebrate Lynn's birthday at Tavern on the Green. It was an awesome time.

Then we have Paula. There are a lot of things I could say about this friend. Actually, she's a delightful black woman, who started at United Healthcare in customer services. She would call me for contract information, particularly oral surgery/accidental dental issues, and we'd chat. Our conversations were always humorous, and she tells me she decided, "I have to meet this woman." She eventually worked in provider services and finally in Subrogation, wheeling and dealing with attorneys and members. She too is very intelligent, has a lot of common sense (which I need from her many times), and is a strong Christian. This fuels and strengthens my own faith. Paula had to leave UHC long before retirement age due to a diagnosis of MS, which thankfully is now stable. She has a number of other health issues, but she never gives up or gives in. Every day, she pushes herself to do things which I continue to tell her to stop. However, she never listens to me, and that's probably better for her anyway. We've gone to Las Vegas and to Green Bay together, just to get away, and we go out for lunch/dinner on occasion.

Our Vegas trip was unfortunately not as much fun as it could have been because my knee "went out," and I was in terrible pain. But just being together was fun. She has a daughter, Moniq, who's adopted me as her godmother and calls me white chocolate because I belong in both worlds, according to her. She is married to Lamar, and they have two little boys.

She has four adult children and two grandchildren. She has a great sense of humor, a huge heart for others, but she's also very strong. Crying is not her thing, so I'm only allowed to cry for a minute, and then I must stop. What we mainly do is talk twice a day or more every day. We laugh, and we talk about past, present, and future events and dreams. I don't know what I'd do without her. She was there to help me celebrate Chancy's and my twenty-fifth wedding anniversary, as were the others. It's just more unusual for Paula to have been there because she is definitely the poster child for a homebody. Paula is very handy too. She has fixed numerous things around our house and continues to tell us how to do things. Chancy's go-to statement when we get stuck is "Call Paula." One thing she has drilled into my head is "pick your battles." In other words, when Chancy's memory/cognitive deficits turn things into an argument, don't argue unless it's really important. That advice has served me well.

CHAPTER 16

I N 1998, CHANCY AND I saw an ad for Heavenly International
Tours. We talked about it, sent for the brochure, and the idea
had a life of its own. We went to Israel with Reggie White and his
wife, Sara, and their children. Reggie was a one-time integral member of the Green Bay Packers. The leaders were the most organized
people, and they had a huge group to manage. We took a bus to
O'Hare, a flight to New York City, and then on to Tel Aviv. The
first night, Chancy and I took a walk, and I said, "Can you believe
we're really here and walking along the Mediterranean Sea?" It was so
surreal. This was the first trip we'd ever traveled together outside the
United States, and it was awesome. And that was just the first night.

We had worried about the fighting going on in the Middle
East before we left. Elisha, the owner of the travel company, reas-
sured us that there always was fighting in Israel, but that we'd be
perfectly safe. We did feel that way, despite seeing soldiers and even
having a picture taken with some. We saw Jerusalem, Bethlehem,
and the Dome of the Rock. Reggie preached on the Beatitudes at the
place where Jesus reportedly delivered the Sermon on the Mount.
The Jordan River was another stopping place where a large number donned white robes and waded into the water to be baptized by
Reggie and one of the other pastors traveling with us. Chancy and I
decided not to do it as the river was quite green and murky looking.
Unfortunately, one traveler slipped, cutting her foot on a rock, and
had to be flown home early. We saw Golgotha, the place where the
angel appeared at the tomb, and saw the place considered the birth-
place of Jesus. Reggie preached again where Jesus was buried. We saw
the cave where they laid him. It was protected by bars, and we had to
go into and out of it very quickly.

Despite the size of the group, we were able to make many friends, especially Jim and Dorothy and Mike and Joan.

We went on bus tours to shop, and I bought woodcarvings of Jesus holding the shepherd's crook, among other things.

It was so internally spiritual, and it felt like you were really walking with Jesus.

One moment that was a little disappointing was Gethsemane. It seemed small. The trees were small and scrubby. Not the scene I always imagined.

In 1999, we went to Greece and followed Paul's journeys with Reggie. I never would go back to Athens although I would retire to the Greek islands. The islands were just gorgeous. Many from the Israel trip went on this one as well, so it was even more fun. We went to Patmos, Santorini, Mykonos, and Rhodes, the largest of the Greek islands. We rode their taxis, which were actually donkeys, riding all the way up. The houses were white with beautiful bright-blue roofs. The streets were cobblestone, and there were brightly-colored flowers everywhere. I don't know how often it's this way, but the skies and water seemed so much bluer than any I've seen.

Chancy and I, along with several others in our group, decided we'd retire on Santorini. I wish!

At night, we would go to the cruise ship to sleep. The ship itself was also beautiful, had several tiers, delicious food, entertainment, and a pool, in which Reggie baptized two people.

When we were on Patmos, the place where John had the dreams that allowed him to write Revelation, we were able to touch the place where John slept. I could feel the indentation of his body and, in the wall, his head. It was an electric experience.

Reggie did his part to make the trip fun. He would play games with us. It was great informal time with him.

We went to Rhodes which is an island with a lot of ruins all of which were interesting to see.

Chancy doesn't remember the trip itself due to his memory deficits. But when he sees the locations in photos and travelogues, he knows the places. We have a photo of Reggie talking to Chancy as he told Reggie about his stroke. He was very patient with him and appeared to be listening intently to what God had done in healing him.

The *Milwaukee Journal-Sentinel* did an article on our Israel trip. The photo of us with Reggie was included with the story. They put me in the company newsletter in a photo with a camel kissing me.

I just wish I had maintained friendships from the trip. One of our friends on the trip died of cancer soon after Greece. We got together once. Don't know why I stopped pursuing those friendships.

One time, I'd been slowly enjoying a few glasses of Jim Beam and Diet Coke as I surfed the net. I somehow got to a travel site, and I viewed the various airlines, hotels, sites to see. As I went along, I decided on which of each I'd prefer. Suddenly I realized I'd actually done something. I went to find Chancy, and I said, "Guess what! We're going to London for my birthday in July." He was not totally surprised and simply asked, "Can we afford it?" I assured him we could, and we did. It was a wonderful trip, with sunshine every day, nice people, day trips to a variety of sites, such as Stonehenge, Trafalgar Square, Shakespeare's home, Bath (a beautiful, flower-adorned town, where we had tea with scones and clotted cream), and Kensington Palace. Of course, we saw the changing of the guard at Buckingham Palace and Big Ben and the Beefeaters at the Tower of London. We even had high tea at the famous Ritz Hotel. It was quite the trip!

CHAPTER 17

I HAVEN'T MENTIONED CHANCY'S ENTIRE family yet. This part of the story is being told based on stories from Chancy and his family and on my own perceptions as a sister-in-law. I've not been privy to all the tales as they don't talk much about the old days. In fact, when we're together, they don't talk much at all. There's a lot of card playing, a lot of laughter, and a lot of unspoken love. With such a large family, they didn't really need friends. They were a party among themselves, and they still are, even if it's just eating or watching TV. His mother had two stillbirths, and then thirteen live births. Some were born in Oran, Missouri, the others in Decatur, Illinois. Some, like Chancy, were born at home. They lived with their parents and picked cotton, not because they had to but for fun. They had a colorful childhood, and when the eldest was about eight, they moved to Decatur. In Decatur, their father worked at a factory, and their mother did house cleaning. It was a busy household with thirteen children, and they kept their parents busy. Chancy tells the story that he and eight of his siblings were standing in a line to receive a "whuppin'" for something one of them had done. There was also a line of kids crying because they'd already been "whupped," so Chancy snuck over to that line and started "boo-hooing" to avoid his siblings' fate. It worked. All the brothers had problems with alcohol and/or drugs at one point or another, but they held jobs, and they're clean now. I'd met most of the brothers and sisters briefly at a family reunion while Chancy and I were dating, and I met all the boys when they drove out to California after Chancy's brain hemorrhage.

Meeting the girls was more sporadic. Freddie, the eldest, is tall and, at first, very intimidating. We had a little set-to shortly after Chancy got home from California. I'd brought him down to Decatur for a visit, and when I said we were leaving, Freddie, who was a little drunk at the time, tried to stop me as he wanted a longer visit. Towering over me, he was dressed in a sharp-looking white suit and vest. I looked up and said, "Do you want me to bring him back? He needs his sleep, and I have to work tomorrow." He calmed down, but only because his sister shushed him. We've always gotten along since then. He has three daughters, of whom he's very proud, and he now babysits his grandchildren. He was a police officer and later owned a couple of bars.

Next in line is Deborah (Deb or Borah), who was the matriarch of the family after the death of their mother at age forty-five from breast cancer. Deb, as I've mentioned before, raised her own four children, plus her deceased sister's child, and then adopted a child when she was older. She also pretty much raised several of her younger siblings. She was a strong, compassionate woman, who believed "everyone deserves a little kindness." She was who I felt closest to, and we shared the experience of breast cancer at different times. I speak of her in the past because we lost her, a wonderful human being, in July of 2018.

Her husband, Bobby, died in April of 2017, and they'd celebrated their fiftieth wedding anniversary in June of 2016. Bobby was a jovial, heavyset man, who loved to laugh. He was firm with his children and grandchildren and supportive of Deb, although, as in all marriages, they had their ups and downs. I always felt accepted by Bobby, and I miss his infectious laughter.

From what I hear, Sam was a wild man in his early adult years, but he's a strong Christian now, active in his church. He lost his wife, MaryLou, in 2016. She was a friendly person who had diabetes and had complications from that and other ailments. I felt close to her too, and although we talked rarely on the phone, I always sat with her at reunions, and we'd share our lives.

Sam is a quiet man and has a very dry sense of humor. He enjoys teasing me that I'm two years older than he, which I'm not. He's the one I'd call when Chancy and I were having difficulties, and he's the one who made me feel more comfortable within the family at the beginning with him calling me *old woman*, and me responding with *old man.* Sam retired from construction and now has his own auto repair shop. He now has a girlfriend, Linda, with whom he does a lot of traveling. He lives in Peoria, Illinois, but he goes to Decatur often.

Clifton is divorced and is now in failing health. He worked at a factory and is retired. He's exactly five weeks older than I am. He too has a dry sense of humor. I don't know many stories about him except the one where he, Sam, and Chancy took a bicycle trip to Oran, Missouri, a hundred miles away. The police caught them before they got too far.

Then there's Chancy, who also has a somewhat colorful past. He has two children and six grandchildren. I've told you about his brain hemorrhage, and since that time, he's been a faithful Christian, kind, gentle, caring, with a dry sense of humor. He doesn't always understand or remember things, but he makes me laugh, and we've had a great thirty-one years. He's the man I've searched for all along, and the best gift God has given me here on earth. We've often asked God to let us die together because we can't imagine living without each other. I've sometimes described him as "my dad in a brown wrapper," and it's a shame they never met. I think they'd have enjoyed each other.

Marvell is right after Chancy. As I've mentioned, she cared for Chancy in California when I couldn't. We didn't start out in a good place, and that lasted for several years. She's a pretty, smart, educated woman with lupus and severe arthritis, and she plows through life without a complaint. Her husband, Larry, died a few years ago, and I think she truly feels a void in her life. She has two children and several grandchildren, and we've finally developed a friendship.

From there on, I get lost with the order of the siblings, but we'll start with Joanne, who died at age eighteen of pneumonia, as a complication lupus.

Blondie Juanita (NeNe) is married to Alpha. They had two sons, losing one of them in a car accident a few years ago. She's a fun-loving person who survived a brain hemorrhage several years ago. She has minimal residual effects and has returned to work as a nurse, but it was due to many, many prayers that she made it. She calls frequently, just to check on us.

Larry, a one-time firefighter, looks the most like Chancy, although you can tell they're all Clarks. He's married to Joyce, who is retired from a supervisor position at a factory. They've been very accepting of me, and they've visited us several times over the years. Larry is the one I asked for a hug when Chancy was sick. They're good, solid people, both Christians, who just try to live their lives and not get in the middle of anything.

Brother Kenny was stabbed to death just six months after Chancy's hemorrhage. I only met him once at Chancy's bedside, and he seemed like a Clark, kind and a dry sense of humor.

Mae is a beautiful, quiet soul. She's a nurse and has lived in Indianapolis and Decatur, preferring the former. She has several children, one with CP. Mae has raised her children on her own, and each one is beautiful, kind, polite, and solid. Unfortunately, there are so many grandchildren running around that we don't always know which one is which, and since Mae and her kids aren't around a lot, we're always embarrassed that we don't recognize them. But they always come up to say hi and chat awhile.

Curtis. Curtis is the clown of the family. He's a very sensitive guy, but he frequently covers it up with silliness and laughter. He's a truck driver, and he's married to Peggy, the only other white member of the family. He came up to visit Chancy when he was at the VA after his brain hemorrhage. He brought a friend to the apartment. Not being a cook, I had little food in the house, so he pulled together what he could and made the most delicious meal. They spent the night at the apartment, which totally horrified some of my friends. For one of the reunions, he made a watermelon ship with flags blowing and everything. He really should have been a chef.

I'll admit that joining the family was difficult for me at first, not because I was white but because there were so many of them, and I'd been an only child. Even after all these years, I still feel somewhat overwhelmed at times. Being an only child, I'm amazed at this large family. They are so self-contained that they find any resource they need from each other. I'm so used to being the caregiver as a professional nurse; it can be disorienting when a caring family immediately jumps in before I can. This can sometimes leave me feeling lost in the shuffle.

The last sister is Diane, married to Frank. She rarely visits but is always, always there to take care of any of her siblings when they need her. At one point, she owned her own barbecue place, but she's always worked as a cook in a restaurant. She's funny, and I enjoy her hugs and her laugh when I do see her. I wish I'd had the opportunity to meet Chancy's mother, and I loved his dad. He was short, rough, gruff, and he eventually died of Alzheimer's. I recall one day at Deb's, he, Bobby, and Larry stood at the kitchen table and said, "You've taken real good care of my son." I responded that it was because I loved him, and he said, "I know." A man of few words, he nonetheless brought joy to my heart and tears to my eyes.

Chancy's son would come to visit family in Illinois and even come as far as Chicago, but he'd never come as far as Milwaukee to visit his dad. So it was a big surprise when he told us he'd be up here the next day. He brought with him, his girlfriend, Michelle, who was pregnant. They appeared to be in love. We accepted her with no reservations, and we were very happy for them. Marriage was a possibility for which we hoped. Unfortunately, the relationship didn't last, and much discord and chaos ensued. Michelle brings Chloe, our granddaughter, up to visit a couple of times per year because she wants us to maintain a connection. We're delighted that she feels that way and love them both.

Chancy's son, however, is very displeased that we've continued a relationship with his ex, and he hasn't spoken to us in several years, except for a brief call to his dad on his birthday or Father's Day on occasion.

We've continued a close communication with Chancy's daughter, Shantise and family. They're very special to us, but they're stationed in Hawaii now, so we don't get to see them often. We do, however, stay in touch by text. She and her husband, Keith, are great parents, and our grandchildren are smart and have positive goals. It's been fun to hear about them growing up.

CHAPTER 18

I LEFT THE WORKPLACE DUE to depression and fibromyalgia. During treatment for both, I felt a bit *stuck* regarding the purpose of my life. All I was doing, it seemed, outside of supporting my husband was sitting back in my easy chair, watching TV all day, and marking time. Since that time, God has gotten me to realize that my real calling and purpose is to be the caretaker of my husband.

A close second is to be Chancy's wife. Coexisting as they do, they present challenges. As a wife, I can become very impatient when he repeatedly asks me the same question. I then have to put on my caregiver hat and remind myself of his memory deficits. I would like to think I am nimble as I move from one role to the other, but I get frustrated when I'm not as nimble as I could be. Due to the location of his brain hemorrhage, "the joy center," some aspects of the normal marriage are missing. The love and affection are still there; his memory deficits do include saying, "I love you" frequently. This is especially important because of the lack of love I felt as a child.

Joking and teasing are also pretty much absent from our lives. We aren't able to go out with others because his cognitive issues prevent him from following or joining in on the conversation. Traveling has its pluses and minuses. Chancy enjoys the process of traveling and seeing the sights. He enjoys the camaraderie of our travel crew and learns some things along the way. But afterward, he's able to remember little of what we saw. If I describe it to him or he sees it on TV, he may be able to recall the experience. But if someone simply asks him where he went on his last trip, he can't recall the event. He also doesn't remember where or when the next trip will take place.

The frustrating part is that when we have a normal conversation about a challenge in our lives, we get it solved, and then an hour later, he doesn't remember that we'd had a conversation at all.

Some of my challenges are more mental than physical because I have to switch my way of thinking rather quickly sometimes. This is harder at my age. In fact, the mental aspects of our relationship are hardest for him too. He does all of the physical work around the house, the dishes, the laundry, the lawn mowing, and the snow blowing, and lately we've had to hire someone for snow blowing and mowing the lawn, because it's gotten to be too much for him, and sometimes, too confusing.

I do the bills, the doctor's appointments, and the driving. I do the complex arrangements if we go to visit his family or travel, including pet care, cabs, trains, planes, hotels, rental cars. It would be helpful if I could drive long distances like I used to, but I can't do that anymore.

The combination of all of these flipped roles makes our life "the new normal chaos." It makes chaos for our life now. It's like a swan on the surface of a lake. It glides along without you seeing the fury under the surface.

Chancy and my far-flung travels were a transition from the self-inflicted chaos of the middle of my life. We both had been through a lot in our lives by the time we met and even after our marriage. Travel gave us new experiences, new horizons, exposure to diverse locales, and the unique experiences of our friends, established and new, who traveled with us. The experiences we had far from home put our lives in perspective, giving us the opportunity to embrace what was essential about our history. Travel and our continuing growth in our faith experience with God also enabled us to leave behind the difficult past we both had experienced. We could forgive ourselves and embrace the reinvented people we had become.

* * * * *

I believe I've turned a corner three times in the middle of my life.

The first was the very important phone call with my friend, Dale, who helped me to a personal relationship with Jesus Christ.

Second was my decision to place Faith with her parents.

And the third was enduring the seemingly final stroke and helping Chancy make a recovery to a very fruitful life.

It may, however, not be the final challenge or chaos that God has in store for me. Whatever the case, be it a good or bad situation, the Lord will be with me throughout everything that comes.

EPILOGUE

URING THE WRITING OF THIS book, several things have indeed occurred, in the world and in my own life. First, my leukemia. The prognosis is now eighteen to twenty-four months, up from six to twelve months when I was diagnosed on October 4, 2019; and my chemotherapy treatments have gone from every four weeks to every five. Secondly, the world has been hit hard with the COVID-19 virus, killing hundreds of thousands. So, in addition to wearing a mask for the leukemia, the world now suggests we wear masks, gloves, and that we stay in the house as much as possible. Recently, in the latest world event, the killing of George Floyd, a black man by a police officer. His death has spurred peaceful protests around the world for nine days and counting. All of these add to the anxiety people sometimes feel, including me.

My leukemia was found on a routine blood check. I then had two bone marrow biopsies, and my life changed. God and I initially had a loud and very tearful conversation. This was not supposed to happen, not this way. But God gave me his peace. Initially my fears surrounded Chancy. What would happen to him? I worried, cried, talked, prayed. Finally, I remembered the adoption and all the other times when God had been orchestrating events in my life. So now, I just remember my favorite Bible verse: Psalm 46:10, *"Be still and know that I am God"*, and I realize who's in charge. And the little girl that God put inside me is still fighting on.

God has blessed me with a neighbor who knows the head of the leukemia department at Froedtert Hospital, our Regional Medical Center. I hadn't planned on getting a second opinion, but when this opportunity presented itself, I decided it was another gift from God. Here is where I'd like to single out Dr. Ehab Atallah, MD, my oncologist. His knowledge and compassion have made this far easier to understand and deal with.

Sometimes it seems as though I live at the hospital. My friends, Lynn, Paula, Kathy, and of course Chancy—these are the people who have become my *posse*, doing anything and everything to help me. Especially with the COVID-19, the need to avoid infection is paramount, so Kathy even does all of our grocery shopping. They used to take me back and forth for labs, doctor visits, and of course the chemo treatments. I'm now stronger emotionally, so I go alone. Most important, they're there to listen. In the beginning, I used a lot of dark humor and referred to my death in all our conversations. Now that happens a lot less. I just needed time to process things. I feel strong and healthy, which makes it harder to remember I'm not-a good thing, I think.

I've now been placed on a second chemo, which has had its own issues. Right now, I'm off all chemo drugs until my blood recovers.

Also, in October, we lost Chancy's brother, Clifton. He'd been in failing health, but we can never know God's timing, so it's been a loss.

I'm not sure what's in store for my future, but as Tim Tebow, former professional football player said, "I don't know what my future holds, but I know who holds my future."

ACKNOWLEDGMENTS

To MY FAMILY OF ORIGIN, I want to thank you for corporately raising me with values, compassion for others, and the ability to persevere no matter what it took. Despite the pain I endured, you did the best you could.

To my in-laws, having been an only child, I was overwhelmed and intimated by you for years. But your dad, Deb, Sam, and all of you listed in the body of the book have made me feel a part of the family, the big family—the kind I've always wanted.

To Dale, who is now living with the angels. I am grateful to her, who with a simple prayer and the Holy Spirit, helped me to know I can have a personal relationship with my mainstay, Jesus Christ. I am also so happy to have had her as a friend. We had so many adventures and laughter.

To Jeff, you carried me through one of the most painful episodes in my life and warmed my heart when it needed warming just by being there. You remain my good friend and have added the love of your life to our friendship. I thank you also for being the only male friend I have.

To the other men who've come into my life, I want to thank each of you, still with us or long departed. You gave me experiences and increased my strength. You gave me memories I'll always carry with me, both happy and painful. You were instrumental in making me into the person, no longer broken, that I am today.

To my church family and Pastors Mark Mueller and Andrew Steinke at Our Redeemer Lutheran Church in Wauwatosa, Wisconsin. God's blessings to all of you who have always taught me and surrounded me with love and prayer.

To Faith, you gave me the privilege and joy to carry you for nine months and give you life. Thank you for teaching me strength. Thank you for being born on your own special day and not on my mom's birthday as the doctor told me you would be. I regret that the situation forced me to be unable to raise you, and I'm sorry for intruding on your life before you were ready. But I'm thankful for our friendship now.

To Chuck and Sue, thank you for being God's answer to prayers. I knew the night we met that you were "the ones." You are like sister/brother to me, and I appreciate you raising Faith in the Christian faith and in the same manner that I would like to have done. You have more faith than anyone I know, and I'm glad you shared that faith and your love with me. Despite the many challenges, you have always followed the Lord's leading and beyond. I admire your courage and strength, and I'm forever grateful to you for sharing.

To Bob Young, you are the reason this book was written. I'd always been told to write one, but had I not looked for someone on social media to be my ghostwriter, this would never have come to fruition. After meeting you the first time, I knew there was a connection, and that God had sent me the right person to make this happen. Being a writer yourself, you spent your precious time meeting with me on a weekly basis for a year and a half, listening, being shocked, laughing at all my stories. You then went home to write all the crazy stories I'd given you. I edited those, and on we went. You helped me to reword my thoughts and gave me your expertise and knowledge to make this into the book I wanted it to be. Now as we come close to the end, you're assisting me with editing, biographies, dedications, and all the other things that go into a book prior to publishing. Your faith in God has been a definite plus because you could understand my thoughts. Your wisdom has guided me through this process, and you kept the prose from being plain and made it more descriptive. I can't tell you how much I've appreciated your help and how glad I am that we met, worked together, and forged a friendship.

To all the friends, old and new, who have helped me remember the stories of my life. I'd forgotten so much, and you brought everything back—some pleasant, some not so much. Most of you have been big parts of my stories and made them richer or funnier or somehow seem less dangerous because we were together. And you've always been there for me with e-mails, prayers, and memories. We've shared our own personal tales with each other and helped each of us make sense out of complicated relationships and situations. I love you, and I'm certain you'll know who you are.

To my Posse—Paula, Kathy, Lynn. You have given me food, rides, laughter, medical knowledge, calming advice, and most of all, you've listened to my craziness and fears. I've had some of my biggest breakthroughs with you. I hope I've done you proud in this book. Your love and compassion will be with me to the end, but I want to have many group hugs and, a lot of laughs before that time comes.

To Chancy, there are not enough words to tell you how much I love you. You have added more joy and love to my life than anyone in my seventy-two years of life. Our thirty-two years together have seen their share of ups and downs, perhaps more than others during the first year. We've never wavered in our love for each other. We met under unusual circumstances. You bet me that I'd date/marry you—a bet I technically lost, but in actuality, we both won. You are a man of God and have helped me to grow in my walk of faith. Unconditional love second only to that of God himself has been what I've sought during my entire life. *You* are the one who's provided it. You've always supported me in this book, even though you were subjected to stories about my past. A major thank you for choosing me!

To Jesus Christ, my Lord and Savior, thank you for your love and forgiveness. Thank you for sending someone into my life to tell me I could have a personal relationship with you. Thank you for protecting me when protection was the last thing on my mind. Thank you for the life you've allowed me to live. I'm in awe that I'll be meeting you whenever you choose!

ABOUT THE AUTHOR

KATE GREW UP IN WAUWATOSA, Wisconsin, and graduated from Wauwatosa East High School. She currently lives across the street from the house in which she grew up. She received her BS in nursing from St. Olaf College in Northfield, Minnesota, in 1969. Kate worked in many areas of nursing until finding her dream job at an insurance company. She lives with her husband, Chancy, and their cat, Tabitha. This is her first book.